"*Heather shares her story with inspiring honesty, offering wise advice from lessons learned. From Broadway to Wall Street is a crash course in keeping it real and the truth bomb every entrepreneur needs.*"

- Chrissy Carter
  Yoga Teacher/Lifestyle Expert, chrissycarter.com

'*From the day I met Heather Terry, I couldn't believe two things—how much she knew about starting a business and how generous she was with sharing that knowledge. I've been extremely lucky to have her advice and wisdom in the course of growing my company, and now you are too. If you're starting a new business or are unsure of how to take your brand to the next level, read this book.*'

- Adina Grigore
  Founder of SW Basics

"*In From Broadway to Wall Street, Heather Terry takes you on a finger licking journey that leads to the success of her famed chocolate company, NibMor. With tasty recipes sprinkled through savvy business tips, Heather shares her secrets to following her passion, taking risks, and the rise of her booming business. It's a whimsical read for the budding business person and the well seasoned one too.*"

- Latham Thomas
  Maternity Lifestyle Maven, Founder of Mama Glow

"*Heather K. Terry shares a serious dose of honesty about starting your own company that will make you a much more prepared and professional entrepreneur ready to take on the daily challenges faced by newbies to the business world. While launching a new business or product can be difficult, Heather's straight forward words of wisdom will give you a leg up on the many out there who struggle with, and may eventually close up shop due to, the very challenges that she talks about here. With a dose of humor and good food peppered throughout, From Broadway to Wall Street is one of the best and most practical ways to take on and succeed in the business world with Heather as your guide.*"

- Jennifer Fugo
Author & Founder of Gluten Free School

"*Heather's incredible story is both inspirational and informative. Her deliciously healthy recipes create perfect breaks in her well written, easy-to-digest stories filled with spot on advice for budding entrepreneurs.*"

- Julia Dzafic
Founder of LemonStripes.com

"*Such an inspiring and honest look at life behind-the-scenes at one of my favorite companies. Heather is a passionate businesswomen who has learned that keys to a successful (and sweet) life are self-love, self-care and self-worth. I can't wait to implement Heather's helpful tips into my own business. I will always be Nibmors #1 fan. "Indulge mindfully" when eating chocolate and "indulge mindfully" when conducting a business - yes, yes, yes!*"

- Arielle Haspell
Founder of Be Well with Arielle

From Broadway to Wallstreet

Cautionary Tales of an Unlikely Entrepreneur

HEATHER K. TERRY

Founder of NibMor Chocolate

Published By:

www.PromotingNaturalHealth.com

From Broadway to Wallstreet

Cautionary Tales of an Unlikely Entrepreneur

HEATHER K. TERRY

Founder of NibMor Chocolate

From Broadway to Wallstreet

By Heathery K. Terry

The content of this book is for general instruction only. Each person's physical and emotional condition is unique. The instruction in this book is not intended to replace or interrupt the reader's relationship with a physician or other professional. Please consult your doctor for matters pertaining to your specific health and diet.

To contact the publisher, visit
www.PromotingNaturalHealth.com

Printed in the United States of America
ISBN-10: 0990646289
ISBN-13: 978-0-9906462-8-0

Dedication

For my late father, Richard F. Kendzierski,

who would have thought this was an excellent plan B.

And my daughter, Magdalena. Know that girls can do anything.

Contents

Foreward

I never dreamed of becoming a business person.

My destiny was going to involve bright lights. And a live audience.

The stage.

All eyes were going to be on me. I was destined to become a star.

I sang and acted my way to one of the top graduate acting programs in the United States.

I don't have a business degree. I have a Master of Fine Arts in Acting. So how the hell did I end up owning a chocolate company? Good question.

There's this interesting phenomenon happening these days. It seems that more people than ever are becoming unlikely entrepreneurs. I am one of them. I found a solution to a problem, and I took it to market.

It's no great secret that I had absolutely no idea what I was doing in 2009 when I founded NibMor. My first two years in Start-Up Land were a whirlwind of excitement, dampened slightly by my learning curve. In retrospect, there were many things I'd have done differently. And that, my friend, is why you're reading this right now.

Earning your MBA on the job comes with its challenges, but it's not impossible and there are certainly benefits. (For instance, I'm not paying back more student loans. Snap!)

There are hundreds of people like me out there. Because you're reading this, you're most likely one of them. And as cliché as it sounds, if I can do it, you can do it.

My hope is that, by reading my story, you'll learn something about starting the company you're dreaming of and you'll avoid making some of the mistakes that I did along the way.

Since my life has been dominated by food over the years, it's only fitting that you should have something delicious to enjoy along with my story. I've included one delicious recipe with each chapter. ('Cause a girl has got to eat!)

ONE

Off Broadway

My parents have always been hard working people. My mother was a first generation Polish immigrant to the U.S. and my father was second generation Polish. My father worked in a steel mill when I was growing up. He was on the second shift, working during the night, on the production line. My mother cleaned houses. They worked hard to provide for me and my sister and all they wanted was for us to have an easier go of it than they did.

In college, I minored in music and majored in theatre. I had always dreamed of singing and acting and made doing so my main goal in life. My mom wanted me to follow my dreams! So did my dad, but he was worried about me when I decided to pursue the Arts. He was afraid that I wouldn't be able to earn a good living.

My dad was very happy when I went on to grad school where I earned my Master of Fine Arts (MFA). He always said that with that degree, if all else failed, I could teach. This became my philosophy too.

If graduate school doesn't kill you (which typically, it doesn't), it will make you stronger. Clearly, I'm still alive. I'm stronger for the experience. And for me, grad school truly was a defining period in my life.

I came out of school with an agent and a manager which, for an upstart actor, is a great way to start. I moved from the suburbs of Chicago to New Jersey to New York City with full intentions of becoming the next big thing. I was on my way.

I was primed and ready to go. But I was also very green. It took me a long time to get comfortable in that world—the world outside the "comfort" of school. When you're going for pilots at ABC, NBC, HBO and CBS, it's a strange mixture of pressure and fantasy. You think to yourself, *If I get this role, my life will change.* And, just like when you buy a lottery ticket, you have that secret moment when you think, *This is IT, it's going to happen!* Every single time. And every single time your heart breaks a little (or a lot) when it doesn't. And then you go to the next audition. Rinse, repeat.

It's a lot to take in. Especially when so much of your success depends on whether you have "the look" that a casting director is looking for at any given time. It really is about being in the right place at the right time. Knowing a few key people doesn't hurt either.

So, there I was, in Manhattan with a dream, a degree and an agent. I was trying to pay off the credit card debt I'd racked up while in graduate school so I had to hold down a full-time job. I was working my behind off in a spa (for a lunatic boss—imagine Meryl Streep in The Devil Wears Prada with a facial steam machine and an extractor tool) during the day (forty hours a week), waiting tables at night (until 2 or 3am), and sneaking out to auditions whenever I possibly could (imagine what I looked like after working all those freaking hours). The other girls at the spa would cover for me, which couldn't have been easy because I worked the front desk. Those gals put their necks out there for me and I will always be grateful.

That was life in The Big Apple. And I was doing it.

But I was exhausted, and that exhaustion was spilling into my artistic work. I knew I had to somehow have one job, not two or three, and one where I could earn serious cash. It had to be at night because I needed to have my days free for auditions. I ended up completely falling into a job at the upscale Stone Rose Lounge which allowed me to quit the job at the spa and the other cocktail waitressing gig I'd been holding down.

My new job allowed me to have my days free for auditions and I went on many each week. The agent that represented me was excellent and I did quite well there. You may have seen me in commercials (AT&T, Neutrogena, Nicorette Gum, etc.), some TV shows (perhaps you've heard of All My Children or Law & Order?), and I actually (cue the halleluiah music) made it to Broadway. I landed a job as an understudy in a play at the Walter Kerr Theatre. That was a big deal. I quit waiting tables completely since I had to be able to go on stage at a moment's notice.

I spent five months working on that show hoping that one of the ladies I was covering would take ill, be called away on a bigger job, or drop dead. Okay, death is a little strong, but definitely a nasty stomach bug that required proximity to a bathroom and an Imodium smoothie.

I actually did get on stage several times and that was one of the greatest thrills of my life. Being up on that stage in front of a captive audience . . . it was like nothing else. Literally a dream come true.

I hit every milestone I wanted to in my acting career. (Aside from becoming the next Angelina Jolie, but ya can't have everything, ya know?) I'm grateful for the opportunities I was given. But the majority of the work I was doing was vapid and I was finding it difficult to rationalize the very expensive degree I'd invested in. I mean, working on a soap opera was fun and I am grateful for that experience. And doing a Broadway show was amazing. After all, I was in it for the Art. But something was still missing.

I became an actor because I wanted to tell stories. I wanted to influence people and to make them think about their lives. But the year was 2009 and a funny thing was happening. The economic downturn meant that work was increasingly hard to come by, particularly as big screen stars started focusing on the stage. Likewise, reality TV, much cheaper than scripted shows with unionized actors, had become huge. The entertainment landscape was changing, fast.

Lesson #1 Your Life Experiences will Serve You

Before I graduated (in 2004), being an actor was a different experience than it is now. Before YouTube (created in 2005), before the dominance of reality TV, and before social media became a vehicle for everyone to try and get noticed, acting was different. It was still for artsy weirdos who followed different methods, but it was pioneered by people with mostly consonants in their names.

It quickly became less about creating Art and more about getting that fifteen minutes of fame. Or, maybe it was always that way and I was too much of an idealist. The point is, my bubble burst.

After spending seven years in the industry, I started to tire of it.

Besides that lack of artistry I'd been craving, I was tired and spiritually drained. I needed something new. I wasn't sure anymore that acting was what I wanted to do with my life. That was scary as Hell. (And maybe you, my dear friend, are having a similar realization with whatever it is that is happening in your life.)

I was burnt out from the late hours. Constantly getting "so close" to the big jobs and being passed over. Time and time again. I honestly couldn't take it anymore. Getting that close to many projects wore me down and made me question my self-worth. I started drinking a lot. It was easy with the bar-restaurant party scene that surrounded me.

But soon, I was no longer drinking just for social reasons. I was drinking to drown my sorrows. To become someone else. To escape. To forget for just a little while.

The acting world is hard. I dreamed of being the next Mary Louise Parker (or whoever, I idolized so many). I wanted to be that girl who got the gritty roles. I wanted to play the heroin addict who lived on the street then turned her life around. Those were the kinds of roles I wanted, but those weren't the roles I was getting. In reality, those types of characters were not me. I know that now, now that I have some perspective. I see now that I should have been going out for the straight laced lawyer roles. That was me. I was cut out to play the role of the heroin addict's sister who helped get her off the street. That's the reality of it. Of course, I couldn't see that then. I was just disappointed in myself. I was insecure and I was really struggling to be that "real" artist. I was dressing in these ridiculous clothes and I was trying to be someone else.

Under the influence, I did things I am now quite embarrassed of. I was blacking out. I was drinking by myself. I was a mess. My drinking was out of control until I had my worst night. I went on a varsity bender. While I'll never remember how many vodkas I downed, I do know that I was still drunk when I showed up to work the next night. Anyone who has gotten sick from drinking knows how horrible it can be, and the vows it can inspire (however brief). This was worse than that. Way worse than that. This was the difference between feeling like death and thinking you might actually die. A concerned co-worker stuffed me in a cab. I can remember laying down in the back and calling my mom, crying. I found my rock bottom and I got sober.

Despite whatever brushes with fame I'd had, I realized that becoming a big star could not bring me happiness. I'd devoted years and years to this singular goal, and it was both sad and terrifying to let it go. I made up my mind to find something else to fulfill me. However daunting that seemed, this much I knew: No matter how bad things were, nothing would ever be as bad as my worst day. I always have that reminder of that day and how nothing can ever make me feel that bad.

The reason I share this story is so that you know you should not discount any experience that you've had on your journey to entrepreneurship. Everything is a part of the journey. Everything is valid and is an experience you take with you. My sobriety was about me getting good and real with myself. In business, I can very easily say, okay everyone, let's just stop dancing around here. Say what you want to say. Let's get good and real. I know how strong I am. I got sober and I set the tone for the rest of my life. I learned that I could be resilient.

When I stopped drinking, I got myself incredibly healthy. I started running 5Ks, 10Ks, and half marathons. I gave up sugar and packaged foods. I began to take care of myself and I started feeling great. I was so happy with my lifestyle change that I knew I wanted to help others find a path to health and wellness. That's what brought me to the Institute for Integrative Nutrition (IIN).

Through my classes there and through my sobriety, I finally started to feel clear headed and balanced. I thought that this might be what I wanted to do with my life. (Maybe.)

While attending IIN, I was still working on my Broadway show, but I started teaching cooking classes from my apartment with my dear friend, Jennifer Fugo. We created this beautiful open space where we taught women how to cook real, simple, basic food. I started gaining a following as a cooking instructor and I was really enjoying it. I started to feel more fulfilled than I had been as an actor.

It became clear to me that acting was no longer my big dream. I had new dreams.

Jennifer Fugo once said that we have different dreams in our lives—dreams of our youth and dreams of our adulthood. The dream of my youth involved me being the next Mary Louise Parker. But my dream as an adult was to make a difference in this world by influencing people to lead better lives. I wasn't sure how yet, but the seed was planted.

My adult dream has seen me building a company that connects with consumers and gets them thinking about the choices they make for their health and in their lives. A company that stands for the empowerment of women (and chocolate). One that has had me mentioned on Forbes.com and living a life I never thought I'd be living.

If I'd stayed on the acting path, could I have been the next big star? Maybe. But I may have also ended up at the bottom of a bottle for the rest of my days.

Now, I am in a position to influence people through my product, my writing and my speaking. And that, my friends, is an even bigger thrill than being on center stage in a Broadway production. (Or at least it's really close.)

So, speaking of Broadway, I guess it's time to talk about how I went from there to here. The longer version, anyway.

Super Chocolate Brownies Recipe

Because you've bought this book, I consider us to be friends. Well, friends who have never met, talked or hung out at a boring party or anything. But you bought my book, and I am grateful for that, friend. And because we're friends, I want to share my favorite brownie recipe with you. Because most, if not ALL, of my friends have enjoyed the fruits of my brownie labor.

Let's just tell the truth. Brownies are amazing when watching The Bachelor, going over to your BFF's and, of course, while reading about how to start a business.

Ingredients:
½ cup melted butter, unsalted
1 cup coconut palm sugar
2 eggs
1 tsp vanilla
2 pinches fine sea salt
½ cup all purpose flour
½ cup cocoa powder
¼ tsp baking powder
5 broken NibMor Daily Dose of Dark Squares (in any flavor that excites you)

Method:
Preheat oven to 350°F. Grease a brownie pan with butter (or coconut oil). Mix the butter, sugar, eggs, vanilla and sea salt together. When well combined, add the flour, cocoa powder and baking powder. When the mixture looks smooth, add in the chunks of chocolate, mix it all up one more time, and place in the oven for 20–25 minutes. Prepare for amazing happiness for all who

consume!

I love how these brownies are so moist and chocolatey. They are perfect with a cup of good, strong coffee.

TWO

NibMor is Born

When I stopped drinking, I had to keep a safe distance from the types of social environments that I knew would put my sobriety in jeopardy.

I was trying to remove myself as much as possible from my drinking friends, so I opened my mind to new opportunities during this time.

I'd made a new friend at IIN, Jennifer Love, and we'd hit it off. Jennifer received an invitation to attend an event in the city that was being hosted by some niche chocolate makers. I thought it sounded pretty interesting, so we decided to go together.

When we got there, it was a bizarre scene—a little nutty sort of random and not my kind of thing at all. It was like I'd taken a time machine back to the sixties, or traveled to Portland, or both. There was incense and a drumming circle. It was not the type of environment I understand, but whatever! We went with it and enjoyed ourselves. Not in a free love freaky kind of way, but we had a good time and got to try some new kinds of chocolates.

The next day, I wanted some of the chocolate I had tried the night before. When I got to the store, I was absolutely sticker shocked. I practically had to take out a thirty year fixed mortgage to finance one of these not-so-free love bars.

Here it was, this great raw, organic, vegan chocolate made by hippies, but it was insanely expensive. The people who started these chocolate companies were all like, *Let's hold hands and love each other*, yet they were creating products that weren't accessible to most customers.

And that's what sparked my interest in making chocolate. I mean, how hard could it be? I could learn everything I needed to know from YouTube, right? So began my foray into the world of chocolate making.

So I was performing in a Broadway show at night. I was attending classes on the weekends. I was teaching in between. I thought I was heading in the right direction. I thought this is where I wanted to go. It felt right, teaching classes and doing Broadway, but I wasn't sure exactly where all of this was taking me—the acting, the cooking, the nutrition school.

In the meantime, I was experimenting A LOT with chocolate. I was determined to make chocolate just as good as the stuff I had sampled at that crazy hippie party. Since I was on a new health kick, I was trying to make chocolate with Agave nectar. (Spoiler: That is a very hard thing to do.)

There were a lot of failures along the way, but through much trial and error (and about five pounds), I eventually developed a chocolate recipe that was pretty good. I brought samples for my cast members to try and they all loved it. More than one person suggested I try and bring my recipe to market. As I mentioned before, I'd never thought of starting a business, but my wheels were starting to spin.

I asked Jennifer to try my chocolate. When she did, her eyes lit up. The cool thing was that she had some business experience. She said she could help me bring the chocolate to market. She suggested we think about going into business together.

I hadn't thought about this . . . about the idea of somebody helping me. A partner would make going into business easier, right?

Wow! I thought. Here's a woman with business experience. Why would I say *no* to this? And by nature, as an actor, I like to collaborate with others to help get a bigger idea out in to the world. It was a good fit.

So, we started working together. Jennifer and I developed the concept for NibMor in my kitchen. In her kitchen. On the phone. In random meetings. On my cell phone while I was hiding in my dressing room waiting for one of the ladies I was understudying to get the bubonic plague, etc.

After the Broadway show closed, I kept going out for auditions and I kept my agent for a little while longer. But in the meantime, I'd made the decision to move forward with this business partnership.

In April of 2009, we got a lawyer, developed a business plan, and invested a bunch of our own money to start NibMor. By August, we were selling chocolate bars.

I was hardcore working on the actual chocolate recipe while Jennifer focused on sales. NibMor was doing well, and I wasn't landing any acting jobs. The Universe basically made the decision for me to stop acting and focus on the business. Well, the Universe and my agent, Erin. She sat me down and said, "You know, I don't think your heart is in this anymore." And she was right. I was very grateful for that agency for sticking by me and for making it a bit easier to say goodbye to that dream I'd had my entire life, to pursue this new dream.

For the first couple of weeks after my agent let me off the hook, it felt like a honeymoon. I was free! It felt amazing. But then terror set in. My identity, my entire life, was acting. I'd gone to grad school. I had an MFA in Acting. Everyone that I'd ever known, knew me as a performer. That was starting to totally combust on me. It was a very emotional time for me. I was in mourning. I'd lost a piece of me . . . something that I'd hung onto for my whole life.

My ideas about how my life should go were challenged. I was terrified but I had to go for it. Never in a million years did I think anything big would come out of my chocolate. I never imagined it would be on so many store shelves. I never thought I would be the owner of a company that had investors. I had no expectations.

NibMor has truly been a labor of love, right from the beginning. I worked day and night, hand-making every single bar of chocolate. We were hand-wrapping each one. We put flavor stickers on every single chocolate bar. Some days I would be on my feet for sixteen hours making hundreds of chocolate bars. Like, 800 chocolate bars. By hand. I was a machine. I ate, slept and breathed chocolate. Literally. When I wasn't making chocolate, Jennifer and I were strategizing and trying to delegate tasks between us.

Jennifer was doing an amazing job selling and, as a result, she was pushing me to churn out as much chocolate as I could. Things were crazy. I had some really bad days where the recipe wouldn't always come out right. As I said, I was working with Agave nectar in those days. Agave nectar is a horribly finicky ingredient to use in chocolate because it's liquid. Chocolate and anything that carries moisture do not get along. There's a whole science around it and you should look it up on the internet if you're interested in it. It's fascinating!

Anyway, we rented a commercial kitchen space that had its ups and downs. Some days it would be great for making chocolate, others it would be terrible. There were many hiccups along the way.

I was a stress ball. I was green (again, sigh) and had no experience. And as mentioned, I was basically responsible for something edible and I had an MFA.

I didn't know what the hell I was doing. I was a fish out of water and to say I learned a lot during this time would be the understatement of my life. There's this one really funny story that kind of explains how clueless I really was about the packaged goods space.

After a few months in business, Fairway had decided to take us on. This was a huge deal. Fairway is a very popular market in NYC. I was making chocolate by hand and I had to get this chocolate to the receiving department. I'd delivered chocolate to Fairway stores before and I would just walk in and give them the chocolate. No problem. But this time, I'm going to the biggest Fairway in NYC which is in Harlem. So, I have the chocolate, and I go into the store to see who I take my delivery to. They tell me I have to go to the outpost down the block.

Here I am with my two bags of chocolate. There are transport trucks lined up waiting to unload what they have, so I go like a pack mule with my chocolate and I wait in line behind the trucks. People are looking at me like I'm a crazy person. People are honking and waving at me, but I'm waiting my turn. When I finally get to the guy at the outpost, he looks at me like I've completely lost my marbles and asks me what I'm doing. I hand him the chocolate and chirp, "See you next time!"

There were many things like this that happened in the early days and I had such little confidence. Another example of how little I knew happened when we had vendors asking for display caddies for their stores. Most chocolate bars come in a display caddy—it's the larger box that holds all the bars on the shelf. Well, we couldn't afford to have those made so we went online and found a place that sold boxes, kind of like CD boxes (in fact, I think that is actually what they were). We could fit twelve or eighteen bars in them so we figured they'd work. We hand painted our logo onto them and brought them into the stores. "Here are your display caddies, but you're going to have to reuse them, okay?"

In many ways, we had no idea what we were doing and the irony is that, if we did, we might never have tried in the first place. And that may be the key ingredient to entrepreneurship—a blissful ignorance that prevents the self-defeating negativity of *can't* or *shouldn't*. That's not to say that I didn't have my doubts—I had a long list. The point is, that list probably should have been a lot longer! Regardless, looking back on all of it, I spent most of the time putting my nose to the grindstone just doing what had to be done.

Those early days were tough and rewarding at the same time. I was living the American dream!

As the company grew and the product got better, my confidence grew. I'm a much different person now than I was in 2009. I was a people pleaser back then and running this business has beaten that trait right out of me. The only people I really care about pleasing anymore are my husband and daughter.

I could list many mistakes that I made along the way and I will add some more stories later. But this book is about my experience in starting a company as an accidental entrepreneur. So I'm going to share what I've learned so far on this wild ride in the hopes that if you're starting a business, you can be spared the insanity I have endured.

The first thing I think we have to touch on is whether or not you are cut out for this crazy journey through Start-Up Land.

Before we get into that, I'm going to give you another recipe, this time for some "Cure Everything" Bars. They will come in handy if the answer to, "Are you ready or not?" happens to be, "No."

"Cure Everything" Bars Recipe

Time for a chocolate break! These delicious, salty sweet treats will cure whatever ails ya—whether it be a headache or the fact that you are starting a new company (maybe that's what brought on the headache). Ha!

Ingredients:
1 cup pitted dates, roughly chopped
1 cup cashews
¼ cup almonds
⅓ cup cocoa powder
1 tbsp maca powder
2 pinches sea salt
1 tbsp almond extract
2 tbsp water
3 tbsp hemp seeds
¼ cup mini chocolate chips

Method:
In a food processor, pulse dates, cashews and almonds until they are broken down into small pieces but not a paste (this is why I like to pulse them—it gives you a little more control). Add the cocoa powder, maca, sea salt, almond extract and water. Pulse to combine into a paste-like texture (you may find you need a touch more water, but you don't want it to be too wet so add extra with caution). Transfer the mixture into a mixing bowl. Add the hemp seeds and mini chips. Mix with a spatula to evenly distribute the chips and seeds. Pour into a 9x9 pan and flatten down. Refrigerate for 2 hours. Cut and serve.

THREE

Do You *Really* Have What It Takes?

I'm sure you've been asking yourself this question for some time, otherwise you probably wouldn't be reading this book.

I think that a certain level of insecurity comes with every business endeavor. I've already told you how insecure I was. I didn't have a clue what I was doing and I never thought NibMor would amount to anything because I didn't believe in myself.

I think most entrepreneurs, at one time or another, ask themselves if they really have what it takes to start a company. If you are saying to yourself, or anyone else, that you feel completely fine about starting a business and you have zero hesitations, then you are a) lying to yourself, b) lying to everyone else or, c) Jake Gyllenhall in Nightcrawler. (Creepy!)

There's a lot that happens in the start-up phase that I was not prepared for. I said at the beginning of this book that if I can do it, you can do it. And I meant that. But you're going to need to put your money where your mouth is and be ready and willing to work yourself to the bone if you want to become a success. (Not literally. Maybe just almost.)

You most likely fall into one of two groups of entrepreneurs:

1. You have financial support from elsewhere (nest egg, trust fund, international Ponzi scheme, etc.) and you are able to quit your job and have the capital to invest in your business.

2. You don't have capital and you need to start a business while working your current job.

If you're like the majority of people, you fall into the latter group and have to keep your day job until your business starts bringing you an income.

It is going to be a slow start if you have to go this route. No question about it.

But that does not mean it can't be done.

You'll have an easier time of it if you take out a loan to help you out in the beginning or if you have money to put in up front plus money to live on for a little while. But if not, you're going to have to be prepared to work just about every minute of the day. (No big deal.)

My friend Adina Grigore of S.W. Basics is the perfect example of a hard working entrepreneur. She has worked hard starting up her natural skincare company. She and her husband both kept their jobs while working on the business in the early years. They literally worked night and day mixing ingredients, bottling creams, cleansers and toners, and crafting individual lip balms. For years. They kept this up until they got their financing. That is dedication. They put their blood, sweat and tears into their business because they were driven to make S.W. Basics of BK a success.

You have to be willing to work hard, no matter what.

Adina and Adam inspire me every day. They continue to work their tails off and, as a result, they got their products into Target. Not everyone can do that, so that tells you something.

I meet aspiring entrepreneurs all the time who have grand plans for their businesses, but when I start chatting with them about what their daily life might need to look like (i.e. no days off), it's obvious that they're actually hobbyists. Or they have a cool business idea that will never hit its stride. The "entrepreneur" will eventually see that life as a business owner isn't very glamorous and that it takes a huge amount of commitment. They will get sidetracked or bored and that will be the end of the potential business. No matter how great the idea was.

This brings me to my first and only question that will help you determine if you have what it takes to make it as an entrepreneur. . .

Are you willing to work?

When you start a business, you have to be prepared to work for it. Have I said that before? Yes. But it's worth saying more than once.

There are no days off when you start a company. If you want to make your business a success, you basically need to be working all of the time. If you're opening a restaurant, you need to be there, bussing tables and tending bar. Every single day. If you're opening a retail shop, you'll be folding scarves and setting up window displays.

Maybe you're getting into something that requires most of your attention but you're still working a day job. Bye-bye good night's sleep!

I was working full time, even at night, when we started NibMor. Was I prepared to do that? Hell no. But I wanted to make a go of it, so I did what I needed to do.

You have to be ready for this to be hard, because it's going to be. Every minute you're not at your day job, or with your kids, or walking your dog, you are working on your business.

When you start a business from the ground up, it is your baby. And like a baby, it requires constant attention.

Prime example. When I was on my honeymoon in Machu Picchu, I was checking my email once daily. Do you know where that is? Peru. Machu Picchu is the ancient home of the Incas and one of the highest elevation points in the world. And I stopped at every dial-up internet cafe I could find to check on my fledgling business baby.

Now that I've been in business for several years and NibMor is no longer in its infancy, I no longer take the phone to bed with me, but in the beginning, it's rough.

Like me, you will also come to a point where you have to institute some boundaries. Your kids will need you, your spouse will need you, and you will need to rein it in a bit. But until you build this business into some semblance of what you want it to look like, you will be working all the time.

NibMor doesn't demand as much of my attention now as it did in the beginning, but I still have to be there for it. I will always have to answer to it. Does NibMor take preference over my actual real life baby? No. I do have perspective. God. But if I'm at the beach and a business call comes in that I need to take, I'm going to take it. If it's 9pm and the investors or CEO call me, I'm picking up the phone.

When you own and operate a successful company, you will never be unshackled. So get good and comfortable with that, otherwise you should probably go find something else to do. Not to discourage you, but that's about the size of it.

Get Your House in Order

As I've stated throughout this book, I meet a lot of entrepreneurs. I don't mind lending a helping hand because so many amazing entrepreneurs helped me. Of these entrepreneurs I meet, it is actually shocking how many do not have their own personal house in order.

What is your own personal house? It's you. Taking care of you. Meaning, you have control over your life, bills and responsibilities. It means you can keep a roof over your head, eat real food (not food-like objects), and generally take care of yourself. It means you don't have a cavity that needed filling thirteen months ago in your mouth. It means if the whole business you've created went belly up, that you'd know where to go and what to do. Make sense? Okay, not too crazy of a concept, right?

How can you expect to run a successful business if you can't take care of yourself? If you can't get your house in order, then you should reconsider being in business until you can figure this part out. I know this is one of those moments where I'm dropping a truth bomb that some readers might rather not read but I'm saying this so that you can spare yourself time and pain. Imagine feeling the pressure of not only your business but also your life? Being in business is difficult enough without the whole addition of your life falling apart. Because, as I've said, your business will throw you a curve ball, things will go wrong, and there will be more than one time when you will think you will have to close your doors. Why add the pressure of a messy house to this rollercoaster?

Five things you need to know before you start a business
(some of these list items will be expanded upon later in this book):

1. It's going to be hard. (Did I mention this yet? Okay, good.)

2. Your business is going to need more of you than you think it will.

3. You will probably not be an overnight success. (Titanic was not Leonardo DiCaprio's first acting gig. I was in love with him back when he played a misfit teen on Growing Pains.)

4. Decide what is the worst thing that can happen if your business fails, and be prepared for said thing to happen. If you can't deal with said thing? Maybe don't go into business.

5. Have a plan B. (Because shit happens…with alarming frequency.)

Coconut Milk Latte Recipe

There have been many a morning where coffee is not just a ritual but an absolute necessity. (I told you being an entrepreneur will test your limits!) This is great after a long night making product or staring at your computer.

Ingredients:
1 cup strong brewed coffee
¼ cup coconut milk
1 tbsp coconut palm sugar

Method:
You can either put these all in a big ol' mug and stir or, you can add ice to a covered container and shake the hell out of it. When I do this iced, I like to strain it out into a glass after shaking.

FOUR

Take Care of You and Make Time for Them

So you just heard me say that you have to be prepared to work yourself to the bone when you're starting a company. And it's true. With that being said, there comes a point where you have to be able to identify when you're going a bit too far. I'm going to totally contradict myself right now and tell you to search for that magical lifetime unicorn that people who have resources (Oprah, Dr. Oz, every single magazine, etc.) tell you to get: BALANCE.

NibMor kind of took off like a dart. We were doing well right from the beginning. I was making chocolate around the clock. But burning the candle at both ends eventually caught up with me. I started waking up in the middle of the night in a flat out panic. My heart would be pounding out of my chest. I would be in a sweaty, stressed out state.

I was too young for this to be happening (I had just turned thirty) and I was scared.

It was bad enough that I went to see my internist and she sent me to see a cardiologist. The cardiologist made me wear a heart monitor for 24 hours. Turns out that I just had some pretty severe anxiety, but this was enough to really give me a good shake.

Do you remember in the last chapter when I said the time would have to come where you would put some boundaries in place in your business? Well, hopefully you won't get to the heart monitor stage before you decide to do this.

I had neglected myself for too long. I was working too many hours. I think part of it was that I'd come from so many years of working multiple jobs and not taking care of myself. Sadly, I was used to this type of punishing lifestyle. (First, it was too much booze, and now too much work!) Staying up until all hours, not pacing myself, lather, rinse, repeat. And it really was physically taxing, being on my feet for sixteen hours a day slinging ingredients, jamming a giant immersion blender into a vat of liquid chocolate and hand-wrapping bars.

My husband sounded the alarm. He felt like enough was enough. He was totally right. I had to find a way to not be making chocolate all night long.

I needed to carve out more time for life in my schedule or I was going to do serious harm to myself.

I no longer wanted to be working 24/7. We were a couple of years into the business. NibMor was established enough at this point that I didn't need to be in the kitchen making chocolate at 3am. It was ridiculous.

I took a step back then and made a concerted effort to take better care of myself. I started doing yoga again and meditating. If I didn't have time for anything else, I would just find a quiet room and I would lay on the floor and breathe. Sometimes, I will just set a timer for ten minutes, set my phone to "Do Not Disturb" mode, and lie there and do nothing.

Make time for yourself every day. Be mindful of what you eat. If you have time for nothing else on a given day, just turn everything off and take a moment for yourself. Close your eyes and breathe. Five minutes. Seriously, it will change everything.

I feel strongly that you should be taking time out to do something physically too. Move your body every day—whether it's going for a run, doing some stretching, or playing with the kids. It's so important. It doesn't have to be a triathlon. Just do something.

If you don't take care of yourself, your body will be resentful and you will get sick. Your business will suffer.

Here is another recipe for self-care:

1. Outsource tasks. Hire an employee. Do whatever you need to do to bring your life a sense of balance.

2. Eat vegetables. And the odd piece of NibMor chocolate.

3. Start practicing yoga and/or meditating.

4. Make appointments with yourself and keep them. I write "Mediate" in my calendar just like any other business appointment. It's an appointment with ME.

5. Book a massage. And enjoy it.

6. Sleep as much as you possibly can (at night preferably). Without your phone. I can't stress this enough. When you sleep with your phone in the room it's like another person is there. It's like co-sleeping with a baby—the phone constantly needs something. Just allow yourself to sleep.

7. Stay hydrated. Always be drinking water. It's so important. I

am constantly struggling with this one, so let's try to work on this together, okay? Phew. I feel better now. How about you?

8. Read something just for enjoyment. (David Sedaris, anyone?)

9. Enjoy nature. Go for a walk. Look at the trees. Listen to the birds.

10. Breathe. Just breathe.

And after you've gotten a grip on yourself, you need to make sure that you're not neglecting those people you love.

You are more than just an entrepreneur.

You are a human being with a spouse, a home, a family, friends, hobbies, a pet, whatever.

Knitting and Other Mindless Activities

I knit. I'm actually not joking. I really do. And it's something I seriously enjoy. *But, why? Why knit? Isn't knitting for grannies?* Well, knitting is for grannies and stressed out thirty-something entrepreneurs. I used to get so stressed out that I couldn't even understand how my brain was still functioning. When I tried to do something I enjoyed to relax, I'd beat myself up. *Heather,* I'd say to myself, *you should be working! Not enjoying yourself, not giving yourself a break or a minute or God forbid, twenty minutes! If you're not working all the time you must not be dedicated to this company. If you aren't checking your email incessantly or doing endless Google searches then you're letting everyone down.* And then I'd go off and do something work related (and not very well at that). I was left feeling like a wrung out dish rag. After working so many hours, I had nothing left to give and I needed to find a way to recharge my mind. Enter knitting, and other mindless activities.

Knitting is one of those things that is actively engaging and somehow very soothing. I feel like I'm doing something creative but not overexerting myself. Just to be clear, watching episodes of The Bachelor does not qualify as this type of activity (though it can be fun). We're looking for something that will help free your mind. Think crochet, painting, drawing, collage building, scrapbooking, coloring books (these are big right now), photography, etc. These are activities that will be enjoyable, free up some space in the hard drive of your mind and will restore your overall sanity and creativity. So find something! Again, you are MORE than just your business.

Sometimes work interferes with life.
It shouldn't be the other way around.

When I was an actress, everything revolved around me and my career. I was so focused on Heather that I would be frustrated if a family event came up that I was expected to attend. Or if my friends were wanting me to be somewhere, I almost resented them for inviting me. Didn't they know how busy I was?

I'm not proud of the way I looked at life then, but then again, I wasn't much different than a lot of twenty-somethings.

I've watched marriages and friendships fall apart because entrepreneurs weren't able to prioritize the most important things in life. Or, they were prioritized in a messed up way.

Luckily, as I've gotten older, I've gotten wiser. When I left the world of acting to become an entrepreneur, I realized that if my company were to fail, it wasn't going to be my business contacts that I would turn to. Those connections would be long gone if anything were to happen to the business, or to me. If something went wrong, I was going to need my friends and family.

You will have a moment where you realize you need to regroup. When you realize that your family will not always understand. Because guess what? They won't.

Family members can become resentful. Kids can get resentful.

At the end of the day, if you have your health and your family, you're doing well. Actually, you're doing fantastic.

If the s*%! hits the fan and you don't have your health or your loved ones, then what are you going to do? If you have your health, you can start over. You can get a new job. You will be okay. If you have family to turn to, you'll be alright.

But if you give it all up and destroy your health and your personal relationships, you're screwed.

Get really real with yourself about the type of business owner you want to be and the type of person you want to be.

When I wake up in the morning, I don't check my email right away. I have some time with my daughter and then her father takes over and the two of them enjoy each other's company before he goes to work.

While they hang out, I drink a cup of coffee, I look at the trees, and I enjoy my life. Before I sit down to work, I make a point of reaching out and connecting with my mother by sending her an email. Or I'll text a photo of the baby to my sister. Or I'll call my aunt to check in.

I make a connection with a human being whom I love.

It isn't until I've fulfilled that need to reach out to someone who matters to me that I start my work day.

I've also shaped my work day around my life. I will work from home during the day, unless I'm needed at the office. I take frequent breaks throughout the day to relieve the nanny so I can spend time with my little girl. I squeeze in a yoga class whenever I can.

Then, when my husband gets home from work around 7 or 7:30pm, we set our phones on "Do Not Disturb" and we enjoy just being together without any distractions. We only make exceptions when we're really needed and everyone we work with knows not to bother one another unless it's really important. That's how I know when I get that call on the beach that I need to pick it up—because they wouldn't be calling me unless something was on fire.

Are there days that don't go exactly like this? Of course. There will be times where you can't control work interfering, no matter how close to perfect you're living your life.

But those little things I do during the day for myself and for my family end up being very important when moments arise where I have to do something that I don't want to do. Because overall, my life is in balance and I am happy. I hope that you get to the point where you can say the same.

As you sit there and read this chapter, you're going to either say, *I don't have it together*. Or, you're going to say, *I'm doing pretty great*.

If you're panicking right now because you've neglected yourself and your family, it's okay. Nobody's perfect. Take a deep breath and start thinking about how you can organize your days (starting tomorrow) so that you're fulfilling all of your obligations.

Let's talk about your battery operated friend. Your cell phone.

Is it just me or is everyone obsessed with a mobile device? Many people in my life are constantly attached to their cell phones and laptops. They're living life through a screen.

I have friends I no longer spend time with because they're always too busy with their phones to just hang out. Sometimes I just want to scream at these people. "Guys! You're missing your life. Sit up and pay attention to the real live people in front of you."

I don't know about you, but I don't want to look back and realize I spent my thirties staring at the screen of a cell phone. I want to look back and say, "You know what? Instead of constantly commenting on it, I lived my life."

If the words you are reading right now have any influence at all on you, I hope you will take my message to heart. Is your work interfering with your life, or is it the other way around?

YOGA, A Love Story.

I was a drunk and got sober. Thank you, Universe! For the first couple years of my sobriety, I latched onto whatever would keep a drink OUT of my hand. I ran, I cooked, and I walked around NYC aimlessly (I saw a lot). I was doing really well but entrepreneurship adds a whole stress layer that started to test my commitment. I had an on again, off again relationship with yoga, but I really treated yoga like exercise. A few years into NibMor, I was looking for something to ground me, help me to de-stress, and keep a drink out of my hand. I walked into a studio in NYC and met the woman who would become my primary yoga teacher and ultimately change my life. She opened up the spiritual side of yoga in a language that I finally started to understand (she didn't actually speak another language—she just taught and spoke about yoga in a way that opened my mind). I started taking her class and a few other teachers' at her studio with every spare moment I had. Crisis averted. But I got so much more than that. I got a lifelong spiritual and physical practice that guides me every day. Through breathing and movement, I know I am making the best decisions for my business (and life!) daily. I call it #entrepreneurfuel and you can follow my yoga adventures via my Instagram feed.

Ten ways to maintain your relationships:

1. Make a real connection with a real human that you love, every day (Facebook doesn't count).

2. Send a card to a friend on her birthday.

3. When you feel compelled to decline an invitation to dinner or a party of some sort, ask yourself if you are saying "no" by reflex. If you would like to go, go!

4. Call up a girlfriend and ask her to go see a movie with you.

5. Set up a date with your significant other. Shave your legs, put on a gorgeous dress, and have fun.

6. Have sex. (Preferably with your significant other. Or yourself!)

7. Invite a friend out for coffee or to lunch, and leave your phone in your purse.

8. Take your child(ren) on a date. Whatever he or she wants to do. No electronics allowed.

9. Arrange a girls night. Gather the girls together and go out for a nice dinner.

10. Call your parents and tell them you love them.

Chocoalte Chia Seed Pudding Recipe

I love Chia seed pudding. Sometimes I eat it for breakfast. There. Now you know a secret about me.

But seriously, sometimes I slip into total workaholic mode and I need to accomplish two things outside of my business.

1. I need to show my husband some love (in which case I make this vanilla flavored with a touch of non-alcoholic vanilla extract or I scrape half of a real vanilla bean in), and he loves pudding.

2. I need an energy boost or need to do something good for myself. Enter Chia seed pudding. Easy, fast, comforting and oh, so good.

Ingredients:
¼ cup Chia seeds
2 tbsp coconut palm sugar
1 tbsp cocoa powder
1 cup coconut milk

Method:
Combine all ingredients in a container and mix well. Let sit in the refrigerator overnight. CONSUME!

FIVE

The Business of Chocolate

Hire Professional Help. Period.

One thing I learned quickly in the start-up process of NibMor is to not cheap out when it comes to hiring professional help. Especially when it comes to your legal and financial counsel.

When we started NibMor, we made the mistake of hiring an accountant because of his low rate. I'm sure you can see where this is going.

Within a few months, we learned that we filed our paperwork incorrectly and by year three, we found out that our books were a complete mess. Oy vey.

Our inventory system wasn't built right. Everything was a huge mess. We had to hire people to come in and clean everything up. This process took years and cost us a fortune. All because we wanted to save money in the beginning. Funny how that happens!

Never hire help because they're the cheapest or you will regret it every single day for the rest of your life. Or at least for a very long time.

If a consultant is the cheapest but they're also the best, great! You have to lean on your instincts here a little bit as well as referrals.

Hire the person who is in a price range you can afford and who will get the job done right.

Look for services outside of the metro area. These service providers will save you a lot of cash because their cost of living is lower than those in major cities. Sometimes city dwellers can suffer from The World Revolves Around Us And We Are The Best Syndrome. That's not always the case, so check other people out!

In the beginning, we had a very affordable lawyer who did really well by us. I felt bad when we had to leave him but, as we grew, he just didn't have the expertise we needed.

When you start working with people, you need to be able to let go when you've outgrown the partnership.

Before you ever enter into a business arrangement with someone, check their sources. You need to know who you're dealing with. Ask for a list of companies they've worked with at your stage and actually call those references. Most entrepreneurs want to help other business owners avoid making mistakes.

Be very careful when building your legal and finance team. You must be sure you're dealing with people who know what they're doing.

Don't work with people you can't afford. Especially jerks you can't afford. I don't care how good they say, or everyone else says, they are.

While you shouldn't hire someone because they're the cheapest, there are also people out there who feed off of start-ups. These guys seek out hungry new entrepreneurs, promise them the world, and then take advantage of them.

I've met some individuals during this entrepreneurial journey with whom everyone wants to work. Some of them are great and I want to work with them too! But sometimes, my antenna goes up. There are big red flags waving and a huge freaking stop sign flashing and I know this is a person I do not want anything to do with. There have been times I've ignored those flashing lights and though I've learned a lot, I wish I'd have listened to my gut in the first place.

Helpful tip: Listen to your gut. Always.

There are individuals and organizations that are going to promise you the world and they're going to charge outrageous fees. If you can't afford them then don't hire them. Plain and simple. They will not change your life.
There are plenty of good firms out there that will work with start-ups for a reasonable fee. Go and approach these people and say, "Hey, this is my budget. This is what I can pay. Can you tell me when we get to $XYZ?" If you can get someone to help you like this, then you always know where you stand. And just another helpful nugget, stay on top of this. Sometimes you'll ask for this heads up and they forget. This actually happened to NibMor with another attorney. We asked to be given the heads up when we reached a certain financial threshold during an investment round and then we didn't check back in. No one was happy

---

when we got that bill! Remember, people are busy and sometimes the message doesn't get translated to accounting or the rest of the team working on your account. Your bill is ultimately your responsibility, so ASK!

Don't lose sight of your bottom line.

In those early days at NibMor, we spent a lot of time looking at our top line sales. We didn't spend enough time looking at our bottom line.

We obviously do that now, but in the early days we were most interested in sales. Sales are exciting and sexy. (Budgets are not.) We just sold $2000 worth of product! Yay!

But we never stopped to question what it cost us to make those sales or what had to come out of that money.

Did we give up 20%? How much did we pay our sales people to reach that number?

Did that $2000 in sales actually cost us $3200? Who knows? You have to do some work to figure that out.

I bet you didn't know this book came with an economics lesson, did you?

We're going to talk about top line versus bottom line.

That big number on the top line of your profit and loss statement is your top line number. You have to remember that everything—all of your expenses—comes out of that number.

Your bottom line is what you're left with after all those expenses come out of that big number.

So while it's great to celebrate that top line number, it doesn't really mean anything unless you have a good bottom line.

Are you bleeding money? Are you burning money? Are you making money?

Do you have a nice fat bottom line? If so, pop open the bottle of champagne you've been saving for six years (or some really strong kombucha in my case). Most businesses will burn cash for a very long time before the bottom line goes into the positive. So that's awesome.

If you're spending less and keeping more in your account, you're doing great. Now, you do have to spend money to grow your business so don't be obsessed with staying in the black to the detriment of growing your company.

But are you spending too much on promotions? Are you wasting cash? Are you constantly having to raise funds?

You shouldn't be bleeding at such a steady rate that you're having to raise money every six months. That is not good. If your money is steadily disappearing, you need to hire someone to monitor that situation and to teach you how to understand those numbers. The sooner you can understand your bottom line, the sooner you'll be turning a profit.

When I was acting CEO of NibMor, I had the pleasure of working with an external CFO. She was an absolute badass. I would do business with her again and again and again.

Her name is Sona Banker (no, really, that's actually her name) and if you need a financial genius, call her. Seriously. Look me up and I'll give you her number.

She was always denying me things, and I loved her for it.

Sona would tell me, "No, you can't do that." Or, "No, we don't have that." Or, "No, it's not going to work like that."

I hated her in the moment (can't I just go have fun on some sexy advertising, Sona?!), but I loved her for it at the end of the month. When I saw the numbers, I loved her very much.

It's like how you hate your personal trainer while you're doing your planks, but when you finally have defined abs, you love him/her.

Find a Sona! Find someone who really understands numbers and your business and hire them to help you with your financials. This person should oversee the financial side of the operation and make sure that you're spending within your budget.

What if you have no budget?

If you need services and you can't afford them because your bottom line is not good, there are ways around this.

Find interns. Bribe family members.

We had to get creative at times with other things too. Like that time where we had to paint boxes to use as display caddies.

Looking back, it was SO junior varsity and ridiculous, but it did the trick and still gives everyone a good laugh when we recall those early days.

When we were small, we could get away with stuff like that and we really had to because we didn't have the money to spend.

It's okay to get creative when you have to. It's better than bleeding your company dry!

What sort of professional help might you need?

I've seen many a business owner turn to the help of a business coach to help propel him or her through their entrepreneurial journey. I've seen people benefit from the advice of a coach, and I've seen people waste a huge chunk of cash on these types of services.

Before you think about spending cash on a business coach, you should figure out if it is a business coach that you really need!

If you're feeling stressed, maybe you need a personal trainer. Or a massage. Maybe your house is cluttered and out of control and a cleaner would straighten you out. Maybe a virtual assistant would help. Or maybe you do need a business coach. But if you do set out to hire one, heed the following words of wisdom!

Beware of cockroaches posing as business coaches.

You're about to undergo an invasive operation. The procedure's being done by a skilled surgeon with an excellent reputation. Her track record's nearly perfect and she's been doing surgeries like this for years.

Fortunately for us, doctors aren't allowed to operate on people before they study medicine for many years. Before they operate on real live humans, doctors must hone their skills on cadavers until they're fully qualified to become practicing surgeons. (Grey's

Anatomy, anyone?!)

This same basic principle applies across most occupations. You generally need to have the chops to back up whatever it is you're doing in a professional capacity.

But, if you've been paying attention around the internet, you might have noticed that there are an awful lot of "business coaches" cropping up.

There are dozens of smarmy people hiding behind splashy sales pages (in which they've invested a ton of cash), offering their coaching services.

Yet, the only business these individuals have ever run is their business coaching business. It's shocking how deceptive a good looking website can be, convincing many people to invest thousands upon thousands of dollars into working with the person claiming the ability to help them move their business forward.

I am absolutely sickened by these parasites who've taken a few mastermind classes and are calling themselves business coaches. How can you help me grow my business if you've never run an actual business?

These people are taking advantage of vulnerable entrepreneurs who are trying to eke out an honest living when, really, they don't know the first thing about what it's like to be in the trenches as a business owner.

If you're thinking about hiring a business coach, I want you to stop whatever it is that you're doing right now and REALLY listen to what I'm saying to you.

Do not be fooled by a pretty front. Dig deeper before you hire a business coach and make sure of a couple of things before you waste a penny of your cash or a minute of your time (as cash and time are the most important things you've got)!

For starters, make sure the business coach is knowledgeable about your particular business.

I own a packaged goods company. I have a wealth of experience and knowledge to share about business in this space because I've learned by doing what works and what doesn't. I know about cold storage, packaging requirements, and what absolute hell it is to ship chocolate across the country.

But I would not be of any help to an online based service provider, just as a coach specializing in online based services would be of no help to a packaged goods business. (Though some have approached me for help and I refused. See my point?)

A great example of this is an entrepreneur who came to us at NibMor to share her idea about starting a cashew milk company. She bought us coffee in exchange for our opinion about her start-up concept. And she did have a great idea, but we knew right away she had a product with massive spoilage issues. This product would have an extremely short shelf life (we're talking days), and we knew from experience that if this woman were to pursue this idea, she would be facing an uphill battle. The product would be unappealing to buyers and she would be in for a logistical, operational rollercoaster. So, we told her the honest-to-God truth and she decided not to pursue that idea. She saved herself a world of hurt by talking to the right people. All it cost her was $10. (Coffee ain't cheap in NYC.)

Do you think a coach who had never run a business in the food industry would have thought about this? No! They'd have taken her payment happily and wasted her time.

If you need a business coach, do your homework.

Find out what businesses the coach has been involved in starting and/or operating (and how good they were at doing it). If this information isn't available on his or her website, that's a red flag, so call and ask for it. If the person has no experience running or starting a business, move on.

Ask to speak to some references. Ding! Ding! Ding!

Once you've found a business coach with experience in your line of business, ask for the contact information of three or more clients. Find out from these people whether the business coach was of help to them and whether they felt their investment in his or her services was worth it. Be sure to ask what the business coach did, specifically, to help them and what the result was. Often, when calling around for references, we're happy with the blanket '*he/she was great!*' statement. GET SPECIFIC! Money and time are on the line!

**Find out if you can get your money back
if things don't work out.**

Ask right up front if the coach offers a money back guarantee. Many reputable coaches will give you a full refund if you feel you were not able to move your business forward with their advice. Though usually, there are conditions under which they will refund your money. Some sort of money back guarantee is better than none. Regardless, get comfortable with whatever the deal is between you so you are clear and there are no hard feelings.

MENTORS, NOT COACHES: I believe you will get much further ahead by seeking out people who have either had success or failure in the business you're in and talking to them than you will by spending thousands of dollars on one of these "coaches."

Why?

Because the entrepreneurs who have either succeeded or failed in the business you want to succeed in will teach you where they went right or wrong. They learned what worked and what didn't work. They have perspective, and that perspective is priceless. Seek out these kinds of people and offer to buy them dinner or, if you can, hire them for a consulting contract.

I have several mentors in the industry who own thriving companies. I bring them chocolate, take them for coffee or a meal—spending thousands of dollars is not necessary. Find a network of entrepreneurs to talk to about issues, failures, and successes. I'm sure there's a group like this in your area. If there isn't? Start one! I did! We used to meet on my rooftop in NYC, enjoy a potluck and talk business ups and downs. It was awesome.

The point is that hiring the wrong business coach is a waste of cash and time and, as an entrepreneur, those are precious assets that must not be wasted, especially not on snake oil.

 Trail Mix Recipe

I do not like little things in my trail mix. I mean, what the hell? No one ever eats those little seeds and stuff! And those little bits of things make up like half the bag! So, I just make my own. This trail mix transports well for trade shows (where you barely have a moment to pee let alone eat something) and also when you're running around with your kid (unless they have a nut allergy, in which case, forget this one, obviously).

Ingredients:
½ cup cashews
½ cup walnuts
1 cup almonds
1 cup raisins
1 cup Sunspire chocolate drops

Method:
Combine all in a bowl and place in an airtight container to store.

SIX

Know When Good Enough Is Good Enough

Perfect is the enemy of good. -Voltaire

We knew we had a good product. Our chocolate tasted delicious and the people we shared it with confirmed our belief that it would be able to stand up to the stiff competition we would face on supermarket shelves.

So, we went for it.

I was constantly working on our recipe, making changes and tweaking ingredients to help improve its consistency, especially as batches had to be scaled up. Our process was more reactive than proactive and I wanted to change that. But we didn't let product development interfere with our efforts to market and promote the product we already had. The product that people were already buying. Even though I knew I could eventually make our product more consistent, no one knew that except for the perfectionist in me. Retailers knew it was delicious and it would sell. They wanted the product we had, so we went to market.

You always want to strive to make things as good as you can possibly make them. That is the biggest objective in life. Or at least in business. To get things to a point where you're happy with them.

In the early days, there were batches of chocolate going out that I wasn't proud of. I hate saying that but it's the truth (slanty bars—wah wah). We're fortunate that our consumers had faith in us and kept buying NibMor products. (They were slanty but tasted great!) We have wonderful consumers and they happen to be more forgiving than I am. Though I did receive the occasional email asking what had happened!

I'm thankful we were in small marketplaces back then because we had plenty of issues.

The main problem was that our recipe was finicky. It was difficult to put out a consistent product. If I'm being honest, it was a nightmare. We were ramping up too fast for me to catch up with production. I was working out kinks along the way and scaling up was extremely difficult. Going from making a few hundred chocolate bars to making 5000 bars? That's a big difference.

I struggled a lot in the beginning. I ended up studying chocolate making at the French Culinary Institute in Manhattan because I had to get it together.

Would I have loved for each and every bar of chocolate to be perfect? Of course I would have! But they weren't. They weren't good enough for the super perfectionist me, but they were good enough.

I had to choose to deliver an imperfect product or to not deliver any product at all. Neither of those are good options, by the way.

We expanded NibMor as we continued working to perfect the recipe. Retailers kept taking what we had to offer because, as a rule, it kept getting better with every single batch. (I had a lot of cheerleaders! Thanks guys!)

I've spoken to many aspiring entrepreneurs over the years, all with wonderful, innovative products, but they're only in twenty (or so) stores. Why are they in only twenty stores? Because they are trying to perfect their product before they grow.

Yes, your product has to be good. It has to meet standards and guidelines required by governing bodies. But, you can't get so stuck in the details that you're not going anywhere, and trust me, it's easy to get stuck there. Also, it costs a lot of money to stay there.

If the powers that be are telling you that it's good enough, then guess what? It's good enough.

Worry about making it better as you grow.

To be clear, I'm not endorsing the pursuit of mediocrity. Rather, I'm saying that sometimes it's hard to see when you're at the point of diminishing returns. Learn to know when good enough is good enough because when you get lost in the details, you waste time, money and momentum. If people are buying what you have already brought to market, then bring it to more stores and continue to perfect your product as you go.

I know our product is the most perfect thing it can be right now. The retailers that carry it are quite happy with what we send them. If we had tried to perfect our product before we launched, there would be no NibMor. We never would have gotten off the ground.

Some entrepreneurs die in the product development stage because they hold on too tightly to making their product perfect.

We get so caught up as entrepreneurs with this idea of

perfection. I have to make this perfect to MY standards. To MY level. To what I believe is the way of doing this. To MY idea of how this should taste/feel/look.

But that idea of perfection can be paralyzing in business. There will be mistakes (like misspelling the word chocolate on thousands of boxes—what I like to call, a hypothetical thing that actually happened).

This doesn't end with just a packaged goods business.

People have visions in their heads of all kinds of things and how they should turn out. You may fuss over how the website should look, how the signage should look, what the font on the package should be (chocolate is spelled c-h-o-c-o-l-a-t-e not c-h-o-c-a-t-e, in case you were wondering).

To tell you the truth, some of the best product ideas I've had as an entrepreneur have come from mistakes. Mistakes can lead to new innovation!

When trying to get your product out there, it's crucial that you realize that the one you have is as perfect as it can possibly be and that's good enough for you. And, you know what? If it's good enough for you, chances are, it'll be good enough for others too.

As your company grows, your product and processes will change for the better. You'll get there.

Managing Expectations

Under promise, over deliver. This is one of the first things my boyfriend (now husband) said to me when I decided to start a company. These words have become my business mantra.

As a start-up, like I said, things will go wrong. In fact, some days, everything will go wrong. I'm not exaggerating. Take for instance, hurricane Sandy. There was no electricity in my apartment or where I worked from, we had several products out of stock, and we were waiting on a container load of sugar required for the production of product we needed—which was in the middle of the ocean waiting to dock in New Jersey (the hardest hit state by Sandy, in case you forgot). There was no end in sight.

I was offered a space uptown with my pals from Yummari (thanks again, you guys really saved my butt and were basically the only reason I got a hot shower for the better part of a week!) and I got on the phone. I called everyone and got to the business of managing those expectations. I had no real answers, but what everyone could deal with (and appreciate) was the fact that I was on the line giving them live updates. As a result, no one got angry, no one was frustrated, everyone banned together and we got it done. No penalties.

I do this kind of thing all the time. Most of the time, I get really far ahead of it and the minute I see the potential for something to go wrong, I start making phone calls. Why? Because it is way easier to manage a situation and find out that it won't be as bad as you thought and come out on top.

South Side Bolognese Recipe

There are some really long days being an entrepreneur (and parent)! Sometimes, all you can do is reach for the spaghetti noodles and sauce (I'm from the south side of Chicago and often remember my mom putting together something like this recipe). I like to give mine just a little extra finesse. Try this recipe the next time you're *'too tired to cook because the business whooped my behind.'*

Ingredients:
1 jar of tomato sauce
1 package dried spaghetti (then cook it according to the package directions)
1 lb ground beef
2 cups chopped spinach
1 onion, diced
1 clove chopped garlic
2 tbsp olive oil
Salt and pepper, to taste

Method:
1. Place the oil in a pan over med-high heat. Add the diced onions and garlic and cook until the onions soften and become fragrant.
2. Add the beef, cook until browned.
3. Add the sauce and bring the entire mixture to a boil.
4. Reduce heat to low. Add the spinach and incorporate until it is wilted.
5. Place the spaghetti in bowls and top with your South Side Bolognese!

This recipe is the perfect example of what we've been talking about. Because you didn't pick the ripened tomato from the vine and cold press the olive oil yourself, it doesn't mean that this dish isn't absolutely amazing. BIG secret—sometimes I make this for people when they come over and they ask for seconds and thirds.

From BROADWAY to WALLSTREET

SEVEN

Believe in Yourself

Things have changed in the structure of NibMor since I first started writing this book. My business partner has moved on to other endeavors. I took on the role of CEO for a while, working very closely with our investors, which was a huge learning experience. In January 2015, we brought in a new CEO and I am now working in product development and branding. The only thing that is constant in an entrepreneur's life is change. Greek philosopher Heraclitus said that. Well, most of it. I added the entrepreneur thing.

Starting NibMor was a wonderful experience. And I'm glad that I had a partner who had some experience in business. But what I didn't realize at the time was that I did too. Because my partner brought the "business" background to our company, I discounted my own abilities and gladly stepped into the "creative" role.

That is not her fault in any way, shape or form. That was 100% on me. So please, don't think that I am placing any blame here. This is my story, and I am simply sharing what I learned so that I might help you in your own journey.

From where I stand today, I can honestly say the biggest mistake I ever made in business was not believing in my own abilities. Not trusting my own instincts.

The worst step I took in being an entrepreneur, period, was underestimating myself.

If there's one thing you take away from this book, let it be this:

NEVER underestimate yourself.

In the early days of NibMor, I was working incredibly hard to keep up with our sales. I was tired and not entirely confident in the product I was producing or starting a business to begin with. Everything was so new to me!

I wanted nothing to do with major business discussions. "I don't know, I'm not a business person," became my catch phrase. But guess what? Every single time I said, "I don't know. I'm not a business person," I was throwing my value out the window.

That statement has followed and haunted me all these years:

I don't know. I'm not a business person.

I could dwell on all of this and beat myself up over it forever, but I've chosen to learn from my past and grow from it, allowing it to become part of my story.

It took a few years of being in business before I could actually stop saying that I wasn't a business person. In meeting with investors, I was always the creative one. I wasn't taken seriously in the boardroom because that's how I set myself up in everyone's minds. And that, boys and girls, is because that's how I saw things in my own mind.

It was nobody's fault but mine that my opinion wasn't valued as much as anyone else's in the room. I had inadvertently done myself, and my company, a great disservice.

Did my partner have good business sense? Yes. Did she have more business sense than me? Who knows? But one thing's for sure. She sure as hell had a lot more confidence than I did.

I did have business experience. I had it as a restaurant and bar manager, as a cocktail waitress, and as an actress. I just didn't trust it. I didn't trust that my previous experience could help me in the present. But know this—all of those experiences add up. Never forget that.

Business Partnerships 101

Get out your highlighter and use it now: If you're thinking of bringing someone in on your company with you, someone you deem an expert, an investor, a helper, or a sanity saver, you have to decide how much power you want to give that person.

I had an idea to make chocolate. I had a product. I decided to partner with someone who had business experience. Then, at that moment, I stopped thinking that I knew anything about it.

I cut myself off at the knees right from the gate. I believed that I didn't have the right to have an opinion about anything.

Don't give away your power.

You have enough creativity and instinct, enough entrepreneurial spirit, to start a company. You have what you need to start something great!

If you're thinking about starting a company right now, trust in the fact that you can make it happen.

Before you partner with people (anyone!), consider this: You are essentially entering into a marriage. If things go south, it's going to be just as bad as getting a divorce, if not worse. You must understand what you're getting yourself into. Nevermind the fact that you're giving up a portion of your product and your idea to someone else.

If you're going into business with a spouse or a best friend, you have to be prepared for the worst. Hope for the best, but prepare for the worst.

Be prepared for your marriage to fall apart, for your mother to never speak to you again, for your best friend to disown you.

People can tell you all day not to make it personal, but it will get personal. It will get very personal, very quickly. Women are more emotional beings so things tend to get more personal among us girls, but it happens to men too. If it's your baby, it doesn't matter if you're a man or a woman. Severing yourself from your business partner(s) is so, so, so hard. If you're in bed with a partner and you end up leaving them, it's like a custody battle over your child. I am not kidding.

A business breakup can be the biggest nightmare of your life. I have seen it happen.

That said, having a business partner can be a wonderful thing. Just know that it can go south.

If you do want to enter into a partnership, make sure that it's for the right reasons.

If you do decide to partner with someone, work with them for a while first. Basically, the same idea as living with someone before you get married (minus the Catholic guilt).

Also, do your homework. Talk to people who have worked with that person or group before choosing to partner with him or her. References are everything and this is a suggestion I will continue to give throughout this book. Free case of chocolate to the first person to email my publisher with the correct number of times I tell you to check references in this book!

Talk to that person's previous bosses or partners to see what it was like to work with them. This is so, so important.

Be smart about it. Do your homework and trust your gut. Always, always trust your gut.

Thinking about taking on a business partner?
Here's a handy checklist:

Yes or No: Do you really need a business partner or would hiring a consultant do?

Yes or No: Are you sure you want to give up X% of your company?

Yes or No: Would you be okay if you were to never speak to this person again?

Yes or No: Have you checked for references?

Yes or No: Have you spoken to someone who this person has done business with?

Yes or No: Do you really need a partner or are you just scared to head into the entrepreneurial forest alone?

Brown Rice Crispies Recipe

This is one of my favorite recipes! There is nothing like biting into a rice crispies square, especially when it's a rice crispies square made with nutritious, gluten-free ingredients.

Ingredients:
⅔ cup brown rice syrup
½ cup peanut, almond, or cashew butter
¾ cup vegan chocolate chips
2 cups gluten-free brown rice cereal

Method:
In a medium saucepan, heat syrup and nut butter over medium heat. When melted and combined (be sure not to boil), add chocolate chips. Stir until melted. Turn off heat and add brown rice cereal. Stir until evenly combined. Press mixture into a baking dish and press down evenly. Place in fridge for 15–20 minutes. Cut into squares.

Share them with your business partner! If you don't have one/ decided not to get one, share them with your employees. Or your mom.

From BROADWAY to WALLSTREET

EIGHT

Stay Open

I like almost everyone I work with. I pride myself on building strong foundations in all of my business relationships. But some people are really hard to get a hold of so a girl has got to get creative.

Take the case of one of our main contacts at our largest distributor. He'd moved up in the organization and had inherited about a hundred grocery accounts. Since he didn't know us yet, getting his attention was hard and I needed to talk to him. I kept calling and emailing. Weeks went by. We were getting a new product in a catalogue and I had to get him on the phone. I was so frustrated. Was I going to have to go Girls Gone Wild to get his attention? I mean, how was I going to do it?

This is where having a creative background came in handy. I left him a voicemail in the tune of The Telephone Hour from Bye Bye Birdie. It went like this:

Hello Mister so and so, this is Heather Terry. Can you please call me back? Here's my number. Again.

Within a couple of hours, he called me back. He said to me, "It's not that I've forgotten about you, but your song made me laugh so hard that I had to pick up the phone and call you."

In another case, there was a particular buyer for a chain very popular in the natural food space (hint: starts with Whole, ends with Foods). This buyer was notorious at the time for being tough on new companies. I remember the first time we got feedback from her and she said all kinds of stuff about the product and packaging. It was blunt and it was borderline rude. I was fuming mad! But time heals all wounds. A funny thing happens when you stay open and don't take things too personally. This buyer and I actually became great friends and she is one of my closest friends. Once I cooled off a little bit, I was able to have a non-reactive conversation about her feedback.

Afterall, she gave us that information because I sought her out and made an effort to get to know her so that she would give us her opinion.

You have to be open to criticism from the people who are putting your product on the shelf. They have been doing this longer than you have.

If you're reading this, you're probably a start-up. You are close to your product, I know you are. But don't be defensive. If someone criticizes your product, you can cry and complain all you want, but that's not going to get you anywhere.

Open your ears and be open to change. If you're hearing the same thing over and over, that's valid and should be listened to. If your co-packer tells you, *Hey, putting these chocolate bars in individual boxes is going to rob you blind*, listen to them. Find another solution. (Yeah, we used to be in boxes and we listened!)

REALLY listen to what people say. Don't get fixed on the way you think things should be done. Until you sell your first or second start-up for a couple million dollars, you are not an expert.

If you want your stuff in a particular store, listen to what they say. Don't give them what they don't want. If a buyer does you the honor of taking your product and putting it in their store, and if they tell you something you could be doing better, listen.

If not, eventually they will say, *You're not listening and we're not going to take your product anymore. This hasn't changed and it's impeding your sales. We're moving on.*

Ask questions in meetings with buyers because they will give you answers. Tell these people that you want to be in their stores and if they don't want your product, find out why. Tell them not to sugar coat it—that you can take it.

A lot of buyers have stopped giving criticism because brands don't listen to them. Guess what, kids? They are the head buyer for a reason. They know what will sell and what won't.

It's not easy for anyone to listen to constructive criticism. I get it.

I remember being at demos and people saying that they didn't like something about my chocolate. I'd get so upset because it was so personal for me. But you have to be able to set your personal feelings aside and to listen to what people are saying.

Trust your instincts, listen to people, and put all the pieces of the puzzle together. Put a spreadsheet together about what buyers say about your product. Review all feedback. Then, you can start to connect the dots—find a pattern. You can say, *I have heard from here and here and here that this is a problem. I need to fix this.*

Nobody is perfect, nothing is perfect. Things change when scaling up. You have the opportunity to listen and make your product better every day. The best products are made when the developers keep listening, innovating and changing. Your work is almost never done.

If you can't take criticism, you're not cut out to be in business. It's like if you can't have 800 doors slammed in your face, you should not be an actor.

Get over yourself. Nobody is attacking you personally. They are trying to help you (unless they are just being a jerk—and those people exist too, you will know the difference). The criticism is going to make your product better. Your product is an extension of you, but it isn't actually you. These people are trying to help you. Nobody is going to try to help you make your product better unless they like you or they think you have potential. Honor that and just consider what they say. Okay?

I pride myself on telling the truth. Everyone in my life knows that if they are feeling like other people are not being transparent with them, that I will be. Due to my history with alcohol, I take the truth very seriously. With that said, there are times to reign it in a bit. When I first got sober, some of my truths probably came off a bit mean spirited, or self-righteous, or both. (And sometimes they probably still do. I'm a work in progress—nobody's perfect!) This truth telling with a hard edge got me in trouble a few times at the beginning of my entrepreneurial adventures.

Take, for instance, a trip we had to a very large grocery account where I proceeded to rip apart the candy set, SKU by SKU, in front of a very influential member of their team. The members of NibMor that were there with me went white! And rightfully so! It wasn't the right time or place, it might never have been. Here is the thing—you can be truthful, true to yourself, and still remain authentic to your brand without smearing a bunch of other people or making anyone feel like they've made a mistake or done something wrong (because, really, at the end of the day, they might feel like the only mistake they made was meeting you). Being in business isn't like hanging out for happy hour at a bar with a bunch of random folks where you shoot your mouth off. Events like the one I illustrate above will follow you around if repeated over and over again. I took some feedback and made sure never to repeat that scene again.

Now, instead of criticizing anyone, I try to have a more open conversation about where my brand fits and why. I'm there to talk about my company and no one else.

The Super Smoothie Recipe

Sometimes we all need an afternoon pick-me-up! Although chocolate is my main squeeze, sometimes even I have to dial it down a notch. Try this smoothie when you feel like your energy is zapped and you are in need of a sustainable jolt.

Ingredients:
1 ripe banana
1 cup frozen mixed berries (organic if you can)
1 cup coconut milk
½ cup water or, better yet, coconut water
1 cup frozen kale (I love frozen greens because they don't go bad right away, or even after a week! For a busy entrepreneur, frozen greens = two thumbs up)
1 tbsp maca powder

Method:
Blend, pour and get back to work!

NINE

Making Connections

One of the first things you're going to focus on when you start your business is making connections. Connecting and networking is the same in every industry. I don't care what sort of business you're starting. It was the same in the acting world as it is in the food world.

I can tell you for a fact that people can tell when you're desperate to connect with them. They can smell your desperation from a mile away. Really, if you're already in a network, you don't go to networking events because you don't care about making connections.

If you don't have any point of reference in an industry, go ahead and go to a networking event. However, when you're in an industry like mine, like packaged goods, you have to connect in a more casual way than at a formal business mixer event. Show up at the bar or go to a trade show party. Try to get an introduction.

There is a distinct difference between being pushy and being authentic.

Why do you want to connect with this person? Do you want

only their business perspective on an issue you're having? Do you want their friendship or a more long term relationship? Do you want one thing or twenty things from this person?

People can smell rotten eggs when you're looking for something from them. These people know you've sought them out because they've seen it a hundred times. In rare instances, this kind of thing can work and you cultivate a relationship and that's wonderful. But most of the time, it gets a little gross for the person that was sought after and then they form an opinion of you.

I've tried to do that kind of networking in the past and there was only one instance where it worked for me (with the buyer I mentioned in the last chapter). Otherwise, I'm not the person who texts someone and says, *Hey, I just want to catch up*, then go on to send an invite via Outlook for a thirty minute call wherein I talk about my personal life for five minutes then pump them for information for the other 25. Gross.

People know. If you think you're pulling one over on anybody, you're wrong. They know you're not the kind of person they want in their circle. They know the only reason you're calling them is that you want something from them.

NibMor employees almost always become friends of mine. It's the same with others I work with in my biz. I like these people. I work with people because I like them. I love these people. I consider them to be my friends. They are people I value tremendously.

After Christmas, I'll call everyone I deal with—my manufacturing partners, co-packers, suppliers, etc. I just wish them happy holidays and see how they're doing. It's good manners and it's good business. I like this person and want to say, "Hi." Simple. But those people will remember me for that.

If you're one of those people cultivating artificial relationships, you have a reputation you don't even know about. People are talking about you and it's not positive.

When you get invited to industry events, go and talk to people. Be a person. Honestly, when I move through my business, and my life, just being me and being a person and engaging—*What are you into? How is your business going?*—that's where I've made the best connections.

Be genuine. Be real. That's the bottom line. People will love working with you if you're genuine in what you're trying to do and you're not trying to manipulate anyone to get what you want. People can see right through that.

Cool Your Jets

"HEY! Cool your jets," is a phrase my mother used when I was getting ahead of myself as a child (really it was when I was about to have a total emotional meltdown). When you're in business, it's almost impossible not to take some things a little too seriously and personally. We all, as human beings, have the ability to take the drama a little too far and let our emotions take over.

I shoot straight from the hip and sometimes straight from the mouth. I've always got a good comeback. When emotions are running wild in a meeting or conversation, I've got to watch myself. We all do.

Cool your jets, take a deep breath, or take a walk around the block. Nothing good ever comes of reacting in the moment when you are hot under the collar. In fact, by taking the time to cool off and separate out of the situation, you will have a totally different experience than if you had engaged.

And while we're on the topic, end the drama! I know, I know, drama CAN be so much fun. But it's really only fun for a few minutes and then it's just exhausting for you and everyone around you. You need all of your energy and bandwidth to run this soon-to-be multimillion dollar company you've been creating!

Try it. I promise something better will come of it, or at least a more positive result than if you had gone down the emotional rabbit hole.

Ten networking tips to bring to your next business event:

1. Always lead a conversation by asking a question about the other person.

2. Attend the event with a friend. (Preferably a well connected one.)

3. Wear something that makes you feel confident. (As long as it's appropriate. This isn't the place for a leather corset.)

4. Leave sex out of it. Business is not the place to be overtly sexy.

5. Be helpful. See if you can help someone with one of their challenges. This will go much farther than anything else you can do.

6. Ask non-businessy questions. Like, *Have you seen the new Matthew McConaughey movie or his Lincoln commercials?*

7. Look at the person as a human first. (Where'd you get that purse? Great shoes!)

8. Follow up. If you made a great connection, send that person a note later to thank them for their time.

9. If you have a mini version of your product, bring it with you! If not, leave it. It's awkward to network with a cake/serving plates/utensils.

10. Be yourself. Be unapologetically you.

Dairy-Free/Gluten-Free "Pizza" Recipe

This is an old favorite of mine that was introduced to me around the start of NibMor. It's so easy and, again, good for those nights when you want to do something but are just too damn tired. I like to serve this with a simple salad of whatever is in season.

It's also a fantastic quick thing to whip up before or after an event. Before an event so that you aren't starving, or after because it's fast. I used to eat this almost everyday in the 'start-up' days.

Ingredients:
2 brown rice tortillas
¼ cup tomato sauce
Daiya shredded cheese (in any flavor you like)
½ cup spinach
Cooking spray (I like avocado or coconut oil)

Method:
1. Spray a skillet with cooking spray.
2. Turn up the heat to medium. Place one tortilla in the pan.
3. Spread the sauce on the tortilla, then the spinach, then the cheese. Evenly distribute it. Add the second tortilla on top. Let cook for a few minutes until the cheese starts to melt a bit.
4. Using your hand and a spatula, turn the whole thing over so that the top tortilla is now in contact with the pan and the bottom tortilla is on top. This may take some practice! Even if it all goes all over the place, don't worry. It will still be delicious!
5. Let cook until cheese is cooked through. Cut in half. Serve for two with a salad.

TEN

Use Common Sense

When you're a promising new brand, there's a good chance you'll be contacted by someone on behalf of a celebrity or personality to donate product for some sort of "big deal" event.

This happens to NibMor all the time. We're approached by some big author or actor to see if we'll a) give them product for their event and b) pay a fee to be involved.

I'm sorry, but you want me to put up thousands of dollars in product AND thouands of dollars in cash to be part of your event? Um, no. You will put me out of business pulling stunts like that.

I get so angry with these promoters pulling this stuff with entrepreneurs who can't afford it. In the beginning, unless you have some crazy trust fund or an angel investor with deep pockets or you are a billionaire yourself, you cannot afford this.

No matter what these promotors tell you, contributing to events like this will not do anything for your business. Unless these personalities are getting paid to do national commercials for your brand, having your product in their event freebie goodie bag is not going to do anything to move the needle for your sales. If you want to do one of these things, know that you might see no measurable results. And I'll contradict myself again because there are some authors and personalities that ARE worth working with and those are the ones that will work within your budget and who will accept what you can offer them in terms of product. These are the people who get it. And if they cater to your specific demographic, the people you are actually trying to sell your product to, sometimes these events can be really worth it. If you choose to do it, be sure that you can attend so you can connect with these end users.

If P-Diddy sees your jar of pickles in his goodie bag at the Grammys, he is not likely going to make you a household name. Not unless you pay him. You might end up in a tweet. Once. But trust me, it doesn't move the needle. You have to know in your heart that this is not going to happen.

Spend your dollars wisely by doing product demos. Put your product in the consumer's hands so they can try it and buy it. This way, you can see a return on investment immediately. I think demoing is the best money you can spend, especially in the beginning. It's even better than a magazine ad. (By the way, I don't care who is telling you that a magazine ad is a good idea. They're wrong. Magazines are dying. Social media and TV is where it's at. We have no bandwidth to read anymore as a society. We are on overload and we want everything delivered in 140 characters or less.)

Think about it. You're flipping through a magazine. You think, *Oh, what a nice looking chocolate bar. I am going to make a note of buying this chocolate bar when I'm at Whole Foods.*

When you get to Whole Foods eight days later and you have 25 minutes to pick up everything on your list, are you going to remember that chocolate bar?

There are not many people who are going to pay attention to your ad in a magazine enough that they then go to the store and make a point of finding that product. It's not going to happen. I know this for a fact because we've tried.

Put your money into getting in front of the consumer, in the store, where they are purchasing your product. Where all they need to do is pick it up, take it to the cash register, and pay for it. Those are the best "advertising dollars" you will spend. Especially in the beginning and probably always.

Chocolate is a horribly competitive space. There are hundreds of chocolate bars on the market and we are all desperately clawing for the same top five spots. This really goes for any business, but if you're in chocolate, you really have to love your product and be willing to fight for it. You must justify its existence and tell retailers why they should take someone else's product off the shelf to put yours on.

Bigger brands have more money, more sales people, and more fuel in general. But I love what I do and I can gain market share by spreading my marketing message one woman at a time. I have the secret weapon! I am a vagina with a chocolate bar! Women want to buy from women! Women want to be inspired by women so I chisel away at demos and get to these women one-by-one.

With our demos, we really got out there and made connections with consumers. That's how we got our sales moving. That's how we survived. We came out of the gate fast and furious. We were making chocolate, taking orders, demoing everything, and going to trade shows. We were showing up to connect with consumers at the events for the nice people who had us at their event even though they knew we had no money to pay them (because they love our product and wanted to share it anyway)! We were putting our sweat equity into this. We did all of this because we believed in our product.

Heads up: When you start your company, you're probably not going to be paying yourself or you'll be paying yourself very little. You need to be okay with that. You have to be hungry enough to get out there and bring in business. It stinks, so really make peace with it.

You need to be out there making connections with consumers. You should be excited (even if you're barely able to afford ramen)! That excitement should be something people can latch onto.

It takes a hell of a lot of work to get something on a shelf. If you like a product from a start-up, support them. Spread the word. It's important and it's appreciated.

Eventually we reached a point where I had to stop demoing myself. It was costing our company too much to have its founder out demoing! I had to be doing other things (developing new products, etc.) and we had to bring in others to take over product demos. It was HARD! But you have to listen to your instincts, pay attention to your common sense, and know when to step aside.

Now, speaking of knowing when to hire help, that's what we're talking about next.

Chicken Pho Recipe

Ah! The absolute comfort food. I adapted this recipe from a cookbook and it's taken on a whole life of its own within my household. People beg for me to make it. It is so simple and warming. On a rough day, it's just what the doctor ordered.

Ingredients:

1 chicken breast, thigh and drum stick, cooked, shredded and set aside (on a particularly busy night, I do this with half of a rotisserie chicken from the grocery store)

8 cups of stock

1 bunch of scallions, chopped and separated—white parts in one bowl for garnish, green parts in another for the broth

2 tbsp grated ginger

1 tbsp coconut palm sugar

Fish sauce, to taste

2 cups of chopped greens (I love this with kale or spinach)

8 oz thin rice noodles

Sriracha

1 lime, cut into wedges

½ cup chopped cilantro

SPICE mix:

1 whole cinnamon stick

½ tsp cloves (4-6 whole cloves)

4 whole star anise

2 tbsp coriander seeds

Method:

1. Place all the spices into an empty tea bag. Close and place in

soup pot.

2. Add stock, green part of scallions, coconut sugar, ginger and fish sauce. Bring to a boil and then simmer for 20 minutes.

3. Taste the broth and add more sugar or fish sauce. Discard the tea bag of spices and the scallion parts.

4. Add the noodles and chicken. Let the mixture sit for a few minutes until the noodles have softened.

5. Add the greens and continue to cook until the greens wilt.

6. Ladle into bowls, garnish with cilantro, white part of the scallions and Sriracha.

ELEVEN

Hiring Employees

When you're in business for yourself, the smallest transitions can seem huge. One of the first (and most difficult) transitions experienced by all successful business owners is the hiring of employees.

Once upon a time, if I heard someone anguishing over hiring an employee, I would have possibly laughed at them and told them to get over it. Companies hire employees all the time. But as a business owner myself? Well, it's a totally different ball game. And it really is no laughing matter.

I mean, it's your business, right? What if the person you hire doesn't do things the way that you would? It's enough to keep you up at night.

I have been through this myself and it's the worst. But, I have some advice that will make it a bit easier for you to transfer from a "doing-it-all-by-myself-entrepreneur" to a "doing-it-with-hired-help-entrepreneur."

What happens with a lot of entrepreneurs is that they expect the employee to care about the company as much as they do. But, really, an employee is an employee. Your business will never mean as much to someone else as it does to you. Your business is your baby. Nobody else's.

(To continue with this metaphor—when you have an actual baby and you have to leave it in someone else's care, you can't expect that person to love the baby like you do. But you can be pretty certain that the person will care very much about your baby and will not let anything happen to him or her.)

The best way to get past this issue of worrying about your employee caring about your business enough is to encourage him or her to become invested. Offer incentives! Get employees excited about helping to grow your business. Let them see the bigger picture and where you're willing to take them as you grow. Treat people well by saying, "Thank you." Small tokens of appreciation go a long way.

Your employees will probably never care about your business like you do, but they will care enough to do a good job for you, and that's good enough.

Identify what's making you worry.

When I was ready to hire an employee to help me with events, I was really, really bothered by the concept. So, I took some time to think about what was stressing me out so much. I realized that it was going to drive me foolish to give up control of organizing trade shows. When I knew that, I was able to address it and to make a plan. I had to simply lay down a detailed list of tasks. That made the transition a lot easier for both me and my employee.

Manage your expectations.

Be very clear with your employees about what your expectations are. I'm talking about writing clear lists of tasks and implicit instructions about how you want those tasks completed.

With my new trade show employee, I gave her backlogs of all the shows I had done in the past and was clear that I wanted her to replicate the process. I asked her not to deviate at all from the plan. At. All. I told her how I wanted her to answer certain questions, how to set up, and what to do on the floor. I explained that I needed things to operate the way they always had. Eventually, I would let her put her own spin on it and she understood that, but this was how I had to have things work for me in order to feel comfortable.

This really helped to make sure I wasn't going crazy worrying about how things were being handled, and she didn't have the stress of a crazy boss breathing down her neck.

Transitions are hard. Change is hard! But when you're prepared for it, things get a whole lot easier. And, guess what? Things never stop changing when you own a business.

Retaining Employees

There's nothing quite like the heartbreak of losing an employee who you've invested time, money and energy in. It's even worse if you've let yourself get attached to said employee, which tends to happen a lot, especially among us girls.

There are a few tricks I've learned along the way—some steps you can take to retain those model employees.

There are three key things that will go a very long way in

keeping good employees.

1. Make it worthwhile for them to stick around.

As a start-up, maybe you can't provide dental benefits or a company car, but there are things you can offer your employee. You might simply need to sit down and have a conversation with that team member to see what that is. Maybe they envision working their way up the ranks, earning promotions and staying with you long term. Maybe they're interested in commissions or bonuses after a certain level of sales is reached. Maybe they would very much appreciate having a flexible work schedule arrangement.

Set your employees up for success and they will do the same for you. These types of incentives will make your employee feel like he or she is an integral part of your company and when you do this, you quite possibly have an employee for life. So, if it means pay raises after sales increase by X% a quarter or a work from home arrangement one day a week, see if you can make that work.

2. Show your appreciation.

Let the people who work for you know how valuable they are to you. Say, "Thank you." Give bonuses. When you make your employees feel appreciated and valued, they will work harder for you. Sometimes I'll give my employees $20 Starbucks gift cards just to thank them for kicking butt on a project or for staying extra late at the office one evening. Team morale is a very important element of a well functioning business and these small gestures go a long way.

At the end of the year, I always give my assistant a bonus. This is above and beyond what the company gives her. This is from my own personal funds as a "thank you" for doing a good job and going the extra mile. And I want to do it and I can, so I do. When you make people feel good, they will invest in you emotionally. (Then, they will have a very hard time leaving you!)

3. Ask for feedback.

Staff meetings are important but I think that one-on-one conversations with employees are also key—especially for those who fill crucial roles in your company (front line reception, for instance). Ask employees how their job is going. Ask if they've noticed areas that could be more efficient. Ask what is working well and what they would change if they could.

Taking the time to listen to your staff about how they would be doing their jobs if it were up to them can give you valuable insight while also making those people feel like they are valued.

Haven't you been there? Where you were in a job and you were dying to tell your boss that certain aspects of the job weren't working but you felt like you weren't respected enough to give your opinion? Don't let that happen to your employees! Start the conversation yourself and keep that communication line wide open.

When Employees Leave

It can be a devastating moment when a valued employee comes to you and gives their notice. Granted, it's much more devastating when someone just ups and walks out the door, but whatever the circumstances, transitioning between employees isn't always pleasant and it's almost always stressful.

When you hire someone, you have to have a plan for what happens should they decide to walk out the door.

When we hired our first employee at NibMor, we didn't have a clear strategy for what would happen if that employee ever left us. When our first employee quit, we were completely unprepared. This advice might help you.

Retain

If the professional relationship is ending on good terms, see how long you can possibly retain that employee beyond the date they wish to leave. If you're given two week's notice, for instance, offer to pay that person for a few extra days, a month, or on reduced hours to help you get all the information you need from them. This would include any information in the employee's brain that isn't documented elsewhere—passwords, contacts, processes—these sorts of things. If you're paying that person for this period of time, they should be quite agreeable.

When you have someone leave you and they were responsible for a function of your business that you have not been involved in, you can't even imagine how stressful a situation that can be. Retaining that employee for as long as possible really is money in the bank. Frustration averted. It is so worth it to have your business covered and to have them leave in a friendly way because they've been compensated for their time.

Most people will also appreciate the opportunity to make some extra money, unless they are going directly to another job (and sometimes they are happy to have the extra income anyway).

When there are fallouts, you do the best you can. If they won't come in for an exit interview, get something in writing. Have them promise they won't disparage the company (though that should be in the documents you smartly had them sign along with their employment contract, right?), that they are not entitled to additional pay, that they aren't entitled to unemployment benefits, etc.

Conduct an Exit Interview

Exit interviews are fantastic and you really need to conduct one of these with each employee who leaves you.

During an exit interview, I sit with the employee and go over all of the contracts and documents that person signed when they were hired. We discuss what they can say about the company as well as what they can't say. We talk about disparagement, remind them of the non-compete agreement they signed, tell them that all emails are company property, and go over anything else I need them to be clear on.

I also try to use this opportunity to gather valuable feedback about how that person felt about working for the organization.

You may not be able to change your employee's mind about leaving, but it'll help you for your next hire.

Exit interviews are a fantastic way to wrap things up with your employee and wish him or her well on the next journey. It really does help you both to leave on a positive note.

The Moral

Cover your behind. As great as it is to hire employees, you must be responsible upon their exit. You do not want anyone leaving with proprietary information, industry secrets, or patents. If you don't handle this right, you could end up being sued or having someone start a business based on your ideas. Though this type of thing hasn't happened to me personally, I've seen it happen several times in business.

Having people quit is part of running a company and you need to be prepared.

It will take you one afternoon to create this packet. Search the internet for templates. Keep it simple. These exit documents should be clear and concise. When you're ready to beef the documents up, go to an attorney and they will be happy that you've put things in place and to help you tailor documents to meet your growing needs.

Ten things to discuss during an exit interview:

1. If you are recording the interview, inform your soon-to-be ex-employee.

2. Go through the list of documents they have signed for the company. Give a brief explanation of each. Ask if they have questions.

3. Answer all questions. If you get hung up on something, reassure them that you will answer in writing once you've consulted with company counsel or HR (if you have HR).

4. Let them know what items they are responsible for returning to the company. For example: laptop, emails, passwords, etc.

5. Get all closing terms in writing. Even if it is just done on a word document on a company letterhead.

6. If you offer health insurance or other benefits, let them know when that will expire (also options for continuing coverage available to them through COBRA, etc).

7. If the employee is being fired, discuss unemployment benefit options.

8. Discuss retention timeline and expectations.

9. Ask them what worked for them while working at the company.

10. Ask them what didn't work for them while working at the company.

As I always say, talk to your attorney and/or anyone you have on the HR side to make sure you are covering your bases and that everyone is comfortable with the topics you are covering in this type of interview.

Kale Tacos Recipe

I love this recipe which I ripped off of 50 Shades of Kale, but I simplified it by not adding the shredded carrot and putting the onion in there. I also like to wilt the kale down in the sauté pan to make it more easily digestible.

Ingredients:
2 tbsp of coconut oil
1 lb ground meat of your choice
1 large onion, diced
4 garlic cloves
2 tbsp chili powder
2 tsp cumin powder
4 tbsp tomato paste
2 cups water
4 cups of kale, shredded (I take out the thick vein in the middle)
1 cup shredded cheese
1 package of hard taco shells

Method:
1. Prepare oven to heat the shells you've purchased—follow package instructions.
2. Heat oil over high heat. Add garlic and onion. Cook until fragrant and just starting to soften. Add meat and cook until browned.
3. Add water, chili powder, cumin, tomato paste and combine well.
4. Add kale until it completely wilts down.
5. Fill taco shells with the mixture and top with cheese. Place in oven and let bake for 2-3 minutes until the cheese melts.
6. Serve with guacamole and salsa!

From BROADWAY to WALLSTREET

TWELVE

Raising Funds

Finding investors is not one of the first things you're concerned about when you're starting a business. Because this is a book about starting a business, I'm not going to get into this too, too much. But since it's a topic I'm asked about often enough, here we go.

At NibMor, we took some institutional money a little earlier than I would have liked, but I'm very lucky that that worked out for me and the company. I'm extremely grateful for our investors. Without them, there would be no NibMor, and that's the truth.

You can't grow a business if you don't have the money to do so. Because I've been around the block a bit, I can tell you a few things for sure.

If your business concept has been proven—if you're gaining traction and you want to raise money—your first step should not be looking for investment firms.

You should be talking with your friends and family members and begging them for cash.

Figure out how much money you need and approach your

friends and family first. You will be shocked at the people who lay their dollars down. You don't know if you have those people in your life until you ask. I was able to piecemeal $5k, $10k, $15k in investments from people and I didn't know they had any money at all until I asked them.

Don't make any assumptions. If you've created something people believe in, they will back you. They'll put their money where their mouth is.

Some people just like playing with money. They like to gamble.

You won't know unless you ask.

My best advice for you in terms of funding would be to hold out as long as humanly possible.

Bootstrap, bootstrap, bootstrap. Make sure your product is going to do something in the marketplace because it will be like throwing money into a black hole if you don't have any footing in your chosen industry.

And that's going to hurt if you took all of your family members' money.

I have to wake up every morning and say, *This is not just my company. I have friends and family members and investors who have put their money into this and I owe them my 100%.* Every single day. That's not something to take lightly!

What's the right amount of risk to take? If you have confidence in your idea, is it ever possible to take too much risk? The world of start-ups is laced with romantic tales of entrepreneurs who risked it all, put thousands on their credit cards and took out a second mortgage to pour money into their company that eventually turned into mansions and Maserati's. And, like any fairy tale, it sounds wonderful—our hero struggles against impossible odds, willing to risk it all because of faith in an idea, and wins! A little less attention is paid to the (far more common) stories about entrepreneurs who take on huge amounts of risk (i.e. debt) to finance their dreams and end up with nothing. I have seen that movie more times than I can count. I've received desperate emails and calls begging for money because the bottom is about to fall out. Thank God I was never crazy enough to mortgage my house or put my own personal assets on the line. Do not do that. Never put your kids' college fund on the line for your dream. Just don't.

Let me repeat that because it is so important: Never put those personal assets that you aren't willing to lose at risk. I don't care what business it is you're in. We did that right. We never put those assets at risk. The money we put in was ours, yes, but we never leveraged our houses or risked losing money earmarked for other purposes (like a college savings or retirement fund). There's a difference between having skin in the game and betting everything on a single roll of the dice.

Never, ever put critical personal assets at risk for your business no matter how good you think it is.

I have seen marriages fall apart in front of my eyes over that crap. Protect your personal life. It is sacred.

After you raise money from friends and family, there are other logical places to source capital.

Angel investors are your next best resource. Angels are wealthy individuals who like to invest in start-ups. Many have experience and/or interest in specific areas (i.e. tech, financials, etc.) as well as connections. For those reasons, Angels have the potential to be strategic partners. Many will have other investments that are different but similar in nature (for example: if an angel invests in food, they may have a portfolio of different food companies). And there are also angels who just provide money. Angels are typically early adopters of your product or service and will not want to take a majority stake. They want founders to be in control and they want to be the support that offers you a cash runway so that you can grow the business with their advice, of course.

I would put a small business loan on the list of "good money" to take in the early stages of your business as well. The only issue with small business loans is that typically your business has no credit history of its own and often the bank will look to your personal assets to back the loan. That can be a little slippery and you'll need to consult your comfort zone as to whether or not you want to do that. Also, small business loans are difficult to get. Since the economic downturn, banks are not quick to issue these without solid collateral (see previous point on prudent risk taking).

Debt financing is an okay option but it's much like a bank loan. You have to pick your poison when considering this or the bank. Do you want to pay back a bank or individuals?

There are also institutions that will loan you money against your existing inventory but it's not really worth it unless you are sitting on a lot of inventory so it's not my favorite option (and it was one we considered at various times at NibMor but ultimately decided to pass on, over and over—it gets very expensive in terms of interest).

However, all these options are worth looking into. You have to weigh each one and decide what is best for your business and what you are comfortable with. Because, believe me, money and where it comes from will be something that keeps you up at night.

The last option would be institutional money (venture capital financing, family office, etc.). This topic is a bit beyond the scope of this book but institutional money is typically for larger amounts of money, where investors need to see strong results and even stronger growth coming. At that point, we're talking about the value of your company (usually institutions will try to buy the equity of your company as cheaply as they can) and the specific reasons you need the cash to accelerate the growth of the company. If it comes to that, remember that competition is your best friend. If you're dealing with people whose entire job is to pay the least to get the most, and you've got a solid track record, let a few of them duke it out.

Questions to ask before raising capital:

1. How much money do I need?

2. When do I need the money by? In other words, how much time do I have on my current path without extra funds or when will I run out of money if I don't take cash from outside?

3. What will I specifically do with this money? Line by line. Everyone you ask for money will want to know what you plan on doing with it.

4. What is my business plan/model? You will need to show this. Google is your best friend if you have no idea what I'm talking about.

5. What has my product done, so far, in the marketplace that proves this could be a good investment?

Funky Fridge Friday Recipe

This is not so much a recipe as it is a suggestion. I am a very busy entrepreneur as well as a mom. Sometimes, the week will get away from me and as much I want to cook that meal on Wednesday (because I am a mad planner—you'll figure that out really fast), there might be a late meeting, traffic, or just a day that puts you flat on your back. Every Friday, I take about fifteen minutes at the start of my day to look at the damn FRIDGE. I look at what is left, what there was too much of, what is almost about to die and I figure out how I am going to make dinner out of it. It is always a hodgepodge. Sometimes a successful one, sometimes just edible, but it helps keep our grocery bill down and the amount of food we throw out really low. As a start-up, you understand the value of a dollar and how far you need to stretch it. It should be no different in your household. Work it out. And share what you created that worked. I'm always looking for new ideas.

Instagram it to me and use the hashtag #funkyfridgefriday

From BROADWAY to WALLSTREET

THIRTEEN

Be Able and Willing to Ask for Help

Once upon a time, one of our employees ordered the wrong thing. Not just, like, a small thing. She ordered half a million wrappers instead of a few hundred. It was a huge error.

By the time the error was discovered, the item was already in production. She was completely freaking out because it was an $8000 mistake. That was a huge amount of money to us in those days.

Instead of cowering or lying however, she came right up to me and admitted to her mistake. She had such integrity. She told me she made a mistake and that she accepted full responsibility. She said if we needed to fire her, she completely understood, but she had xyz as a solution.

She took a deep breath and said that she would hand in her resignation because she screwed up, but here's what she thought could fix the problem.

We did not fire her. I would never fire someone who has this kind of integrity and comes to me with honesty and a solution.

She is the kind of person I want on my staff because she will come to me when she screws up and she will be honest with me.

Everyone screws up. But most people try to hide it.

I mess up on a daily basis. But, you know what? You have to come clean and you have to know when to ask for help.

People make mistakes. If you're worried about employees making mistakes, get over it because unless you're hiring robots, mistakes will be made.

Asking For Help

In this scenario, our employee had a hole in her proverbial boat. She saw the hole and immediately sought help.

Now, imagine you are in a boat. And there is a hole in your boat.

You see the hole. You can recognize that the hole is getting bigger.

Do you call for help or wait until the boat sinks?

I'm going to bet that you ask for help the minute you realize the hole is getting bigger and the sea is going to swallow you.

But a lot of people in business will ignore the hole.

Oh, it's fine. We have time.

Or, *Oh, I'll just put a Band-Aid on the hole. The hole will be fine.*

Guess what? The hole is going to get bigger until it's fixed. The bigger the hole gets, the closer you are to sinking the boat.

Let the hole go and you're gone forever. You're sunk.

I see this happen ALL the time.

ASK for help, like our employee did. If you see the problem and you do not address it, your boat will sink.

Imagine you're going to see the co-manufacturer and the co-manufacturer has made your product wrong. You're nervous to say anything about the product not being right. You know you have to tell them, but you can't.

You let that order go out there and nothing is said. But then another order comes in and since you haven't told that manufacturer that it was made wrong, another order goes out wrong. Two crap-tacular orders are out in the stores.

A big box retailer now places an order for 400 pallets of product. You haven't addressed the problem. Those pallets get to the big box store. They penetrate the market. People are unhappy and your product gets recalled.

Your boat is sinking.

The manufacturer says it wasn't their problem because they made the product the same as you've been telling them to.

You can't sell the product because it's been recalled.

You are sunk.

Done. You're dead.

You wanted it to work so badly that you ignored the problem. It's too late. The big retailer has returned 400 pallets. You just put a ton of cash into inventory that you can't use. Your business is done.

At the first sign of a hole in your boat, call EVERYONE you know. If you don't know someone that can help with the problem, call someone who might know someone. If you ignore the problem, your boat will sink.

It doesn't matter if you know someone who can deal with the problem directly. Call ANYONE who you think might know ANYONE. Someone has been there.

Anyone in your space who tells you they haven't had a hole in their boat is lying to you. We all need help. We all come across problems where we need help. It's an unwritten rule of entrepreneurship that you pay it forward when someone else needs help. That's just how it works.

Ask for help. Give help to those who ask for it and need it. It all comes around full circle.

Gluten-Free Almond Granola Recipe

This is another family favorite around my house. If you're staying at this B&B, you can be sure the Terry's will be serving this granola in the morning.

This recipe is basically my secret household recipe and I'm sharing it with you! This recipe will add value to your life. Make it, share it! All good things that go around, come around!

Ingredients:
2 ½ tbsp coconut oil (melted)
Sea salt (a few pinches)
2 cups gluten-free oats
⅓ cup maple syrup
1 cup almonds
⅓ cup coconut palm sugar
½ tsp vanilla extract
3 tbsp ground flax seed
2 tbsp hemp or Chia seed
⅓ cup almond butter

Method:
1. Preheat oven to 325°F.
2. In a bowl, add coconut oil, sea salt, maple syrup, coconut sugar, almond butter and vanilla until well combined. Add remaining ingredients and stir well again.
3. Spread the mixture on a baking pan evenly but keep some of the chunks intact (they're nice in the finished product).
4. Bake, stirring every once in a while and folding the outside edges

in and the inside edges out for 35-45 minutes or until the granola is dry and starting to turn a light brown color.

5. Let cool a few minutes before serving.

You can store this in an airtight container for up to two weeks.

FOURTEEN

Don't Waste Other People's Time

I had a supplier commit to delivering a product by a certain date. That person, when I called to check up on the shipment, said, "Oh, we don't have any stock and we're really busy, so that's not going to happen."

Can you guess why that supplier lost my business?

We're all busy. That is not an excuse. You have to be able to do what you say you're going to do.

Speaking of doing what you say you're going to do—don't be late.

If you're asking someone for help and you're late for your agreed upon meeting time? No bueno.

Whoever you're meeting with is also very busy. If they've given up their time to meet with you, you cannot be late.

Chronic lateness is a deal breaker. And be prepared for meetings so that you're not wasting someone's time.

Cash is king and time is money.

You need cash to keep your business moving, but time is the single most valuable thing you have to offer as a business owner.

It is SO important.

You own a business. You have kids. You have other things going on that are very important in your day-to-day. Someone being late or unprepared is unacceptable. You only have so many hours in the day.

When you waste someone's time, it is very insulting.

People who are always unprepared or people who are always late don't get a second chance to work with me.

Your tardiness is not cute. When you're late or unprepared, it looks like you can't manage your time, so how can you expect people to respect you as a business person?

I am not perfect but I am never late. I am always prepared. If I am going to be late, I'm texting someone 15-20 minutes out with a warning. But really, I'm never late.

The entertainment world runs on a different clock. When I was an actress, I would go in for auditions and I would sit for an hour and a half past my appointment time and still not get called in. I would have to leave many times after sitting there for an hour and a half. 9.9 times out of 10, nobody would even apologize for running late. Sometimes, someone would come out and apologize and offer to reschedule, but most of the time, their heads were so far up their behinds that these people would expect you to sit and wait for hours for a crappy little job.

This kind of blatant disrespect is not okay in any business. It's just not okay.

I respected your time by showing up when I said I would.

When you're consistently on time, it sends a message. It tells people that you have character and that you are trustworthy.

If my staff members are not on time for our staff meetings, they know I'm starting without them. If the meeting's at 1pm, the meeting's at 1pm. I don't care if it's an investor or a filing clerk who's late. The meeting starts when it starts. It sets a precedent.

Time is money and money is time.

There's a reason why we get paid for our time. Our time is valuable. Time equals money. Be respectful. That is all.

Flavorful Chicken Tenders Recipe

This one is another easy and impressive meal. Your family, friends or cat will look at you and think, *Damn! You are so busy doing this start-up thing AND you cooked this delicious, flavorful meal? ROCKSTAR.* You're welcome. Serve this with a salad, some simple roasted potatoes, or steamed greens.

Ingredients:
1 lb chicken tenders
1 ½ cup coconut flour (almond works well too)
3 tbsp of your favorite spice mixture*
Cooking spray (avocado or coconut oil are best)

Method:
1. Preheat oven to 350°F.
2. Coat the bottom of a baking dish with the cooking spray.
3. Combine the flour and the spice mixture in a large bowl and mix well.
4. Dredge each chicken tender in the flour mixture and place in the baking dish.
5. Bake for 7 minutes, then flip the chicken over and cook for another 4-7minutes until cooked all the way through.

Easy breezy.

*Spice mixture—an all purpose seasoning works really well for this. Also, I've been known to mimic one of my favorite spice companies by throwing this concoction together: chili powder, coconut palm sugar, paprika, flake salt, garlic powder, onion powder, coffee grounds, black pepper.

FIFTEEN

Giving Back

As much as I loved the idea of NibMor giving back, for a long time, we didn't know how we were going to do that or what it would look like.

There are two reasons companies choose to give back:

1. Because it will make their company look good.

2. Because it's the right thing to do.

Before I go any further, I'm going to let you guess which of those reasons is the most noble.

K, that wasn't hard, right?

When I talk about giving back, this does not mean donating a few dollars to a cause so that you can say you contribute to society and that you're a great company for doing so. I'm talking about giving back because it's the right thing to do.

I give back because I am a human being on this Earth who has been dealt a good hand in life. I really believe we have to take care of each other during our time on this planet. That's why I choose to support the charities I believe in. It's not because I want to be able to put something on my labels that says, "Hey look, NibMor is a good corporate citizen."

Don't partner with an organization because you think it will help you sell more product. That is gross. Giving back has to come from a good place. Otherwise, your "good act" is really all about you.

Ya know what? We all need to help each other and elevate one another to find peace and harmony and happiness on Earth. As a business owner, you're in an excellent position to do this on a larger scale than a lot of individuals are able to do.

In the beginning, NibMor worked with HealthCorps, an organization started by Dr. Oz and his wife to help fight childhood obesity. We loved working with them. HealthCorps is doing amazing things and with a celebrity behind it, it was a great organization for us to be aligned with. They were doing great things but they needed money more than anything and, as a start-up, we didn't have much money to offer.

If you're in that same scenario and you have limited money to offer a charity, find an organization or a cause that will value your time and/or expertise.

For me, I love teaching kids about chocolate, so I volunteer my time whenever I can to youth groups and kid-centric organizations. Kids are interested because chocolate is cool! They learn something valuable that they didn't know before and I feel good about it. That is what I did with HealthCorps in the beginning because we didn't have the cash.

I'm sure you can find a parallel in your business.

If you can afford monetary means of giving back, go for it. But don't break the bank.

You know what company I really love? Toms. Toms has its philanthropic message woven throughout its brand. They have revolutionized the "one-for-one" way of doing business. When you buy a pair of Toms, another pair of Toms is given to a child in need. That's amazing.

If I knew of anyone who needed chocolate to sustain life, I would totally adopt that model.

But with NibMor, I want to talk about women.

Being a female entrepreneur is something that's important to me. Men are still earning more than women for doing the same jobs and that's not acceptable. Gender equality is important to me, especially now that I have a daughter. How can I explain to her one day why women earn seventy cents on the dollar to what a man earns? I don't want her to live in a world where that's okay. We are in the United States of America and this is unacceptable.

NibMor is interested in female driven initiatives right now. It's cool because we're a food company and these types of cases aren't often looked at in our space. We want to bring awareness to something that nobody else in the chocolate world is talking about.

Find what makes you tick (I'm seriously hot under the collar right now thinking about the wage thing) and put everything you have behind it. That energy will change the world.

Hand Rolled Raw Truffles

I make these whenever I'm at a school with the kiddies. They love these because they can take them home and they are easy enough to make at home and share with their families. I have often defaulted to these when I'm in a time crunch for a dinner party or when I need to bring something to a potluck and they are always a hit.

Ingredients:
2 tbsp coconut butter
⅓ cup gogi berries
2 tbsp almond butter
1 tbsp Chia seeds
1 tbsp cacao powder
⅓ cup walnuts
A touch of Agave nectar, maple syrup or coconut nectar

Method:
1. Line a baking sheet with parchment paper and set aside.
2. Combine all ingredients in a mini food prep, Vitamix or food processor. Blend on a low level, or risk the whole thing becoming a nut-like butter! We still want some chunkiness here.
3. Pour the contents into a bowl and then, using your hands, shape the mixture into 10 balls or truffles. Place on the baking sheet.
4. Place in the freezer for 10-15 minutes. These will keep in the fridge or freezer for up to 3 days.

SIXTEEN

One Last Bite

I never thought I would have an idea for a business, start a business, or have a sliver of the business insight I've presented here in these pages. But, here we are. I actually finished a business book. Like, writing one. Not just reading one. (Reading is also good, obviously. Yay you for reading this!)

Being an entrepreneur is a wild ride but it's one that I am so grateful to have taken. And I'm excited for you, about to embark on your own ride. You're in for a lot of excitement. Each day there are unexpected surprises, both good and bad. Get the fire hose and champagne (or kombucha) bottle ready.

One of my best bits of advice to you is that you stay organized and focused. If you can do both of those things, success or failure will reveal itself to you very quickly.

NibMor was a labor of love and ignorance. I may not have jumped in so quickly if I knew 100% of what was ahead. So from where I sit today, I consider my ignorance to have actually been a good thing. I learned about strengths I never knew I had. I found out how to think on my feet and problem solve in a very impromptu way.

So, my dear entrepreneur, jump in like I did if you believe in your idea and product. You may fail but, if you do? Then at least fail big.

People ask me all the time if I'd do it again or if I'd start another company. Would I do it again? Absolutely. Not only have I learned a lot about business in general with NibMor, but I have learned some of my greatest life lessons. I've learned that passion will take you places, but it will only take you so far. I have found glaring character flaws within myself that can only help me become a better business person, wife, mother and friend as I work through my life and karma.

I've also found the best parts of myself. The parts I am most proud of and the things I am great at. I now play to my strengths. So yes, 100% yes. I would do it all over again and all in the same way.

Would I start a different kind of company? Well, you'll have to wait and see. A girl has to keep some things to herself. Stay tuned.

Yours in Entrepreneurship (& Chocolate),

Heather K. Terry

Gratitude

There are so many people to thank, I will do my best here. (This is like the Oscar speech I always wanted to write!) Loads of gratitude are owed to the following people:

To everyone who made NibMor possible. And to all those who encouraged me to take my idea and start a company. To all the early chocolate taste testers—some good experiences and some mediocre—your feedback and honesty shaped my ideas of how to create and make a product and I thank you.

The team and individuals whom I worked with at the Gerber Group. I still think of you all like family. Each and every one of you shaped me more than you will ever know.

Christopher Kula and everyone on the legal team at Phillips Nizer in NYC who deals with me. Thank you.

JLM and Cristina, I could not have done this without you both. It has been a long road and you should feel proud knowing that you had a huge hand in helping me get this done. I am eternally grateful.

My business partner of nearly five years, Jennifer Love. I wish you all the best in your future endeavors.

All the entrepreneurs who invite me along on their journeys, thank you. I learn something new all the time. Keep innovating and dreaming big!

To everyone who works for NibMor and has worked for

NibMor, especially Jennifer Stachon, Jessica Osias and Lu. You gals made this all happen. Truly, it was all you—I just make chocolate. You gals made everything else materialize. No question.

Thank you, my dear friend, Scott Greenburg, who has always picked up the phone, given great feedback and is always up for a steak dinner. You encouraged me to embrace my inner a-hole and I'll always be grateful. (An entrepreneurial lesson I've covered on my blog!)

Paula Liberis, I am so grateful I met you, it truly was fate. Well, that, and me continually showing up to your classes like a stalker. You have been an amazing spiritual teacher and friend. You changed my practice and life.

The amazing and talented, Sona Banker. You and I have been through it all. Thank you, thank you, thank you.

Lauren Fahey Appelt, you are the best employee anyone could have ever asked for. I am grateful we are a part of one another's lives. You and the Fahey tribe are like my east coast family. Thank you for your loyalty and hard work.

A big thank you to Rachel Forillere, an industry connection turned lifelong friend. You've taught me what it takes to be successful in the grocery channel, you've listened for many, many hours, you have thickened my skin, and most importantly (especially on the most difficult days), given me a great big laugh.

Adina Grigore and Adam Poor, who are an extension of our family and amazing entrepreneurs. I just love you two and your hipster-ness.

To my dearest friends, Lisa Kolotouros (BFF forever), Michelle Ramoni (I might not actually be alive without you), Jennifer Fugo Gresh (sanity might be questionable without you), Tracee Chimo (we've been through some times, eh?), Catherine Walsh (swear we partied together somewhere) and Almeria Campbell (my second Polish sister). You have all stood by me through some of my darkest days and brightest transitions. You inspire me to create on a daily basis and are amongst the most important women in my life.

Kathleen & William Gibbons, Timothy Birner, and Russell Walther, the first four people to read versions of this book and offer me unfiltered feedback. You all made a huge difference in the direction it all took. Thank you for your time, suggestions and buckets of encouragement.

Tim Rogers, Allyson Myers and Bryan Fuller, who all helped grow NibMor with their infinite knowledge of production and supply chain. One is only as good as the people they surround themselves with and I am so grateful you all took a chance on NibMor and me. You all continue to be fantastic partners and friends.

Emil Capital Partners, especially Vadim Zverev, who invested in NibMor early on and continue to be partners today. I have learned so much from all of you. You've pushed me to my limits and have always believed in the product and vision of the company. I am eternally grateful.

A big thank you to Ralph Chauvin, NibMor's CEO. Who knew I could learn so much from one person in such a short period of time? Don't worry, I'm going to go call someone to push them into a sales call right now. Promise.

My publishers, Lindsey and Amie and everyone at PNH, you have been very patient with this entrepreneur! A million thank you's for having faith in me, my ideas and my words. And also for dealing with my very hectic schedule. Not many authors can say they've had the experience I've had with you and your team. I look forward to many more adventures.

Aunt Marlene, Uncle John, Tammy (& crew), and Lisa, I am very grateful you are all in my life. Thank you for accepting me as I am and for always offering love and support.

Peter Terry and Joan Salim for always asking, "How are things going?" (because most of the time I forget to ask myself!) and encouraging me in every pursuit.

Anne Terry, thank you for your suggestions, ideas and enthusiasm (and the most thought provoking emails)!

My sister, Victoria Kendzierski, you are incredible and teach me so much. I am so grateful to you for your encouragement in starting NibMor and especially in writing this book. You are the best cheerleader on the planet.

Duane Lynn, there were many days I thought I would never get through writing this book. I drew courage from your book, knowing that if you could put yourself out there in that way, then I could too.

My mother, JoAnna Lynn, I love you. Thank you for always loving me and offering unwavering support, as an actress first and then later as an entrepreneur. I'm not sure another mother could have believed in their child as much as you've always believed in me.

My husband, Michael, who really deserves some writing credit here. He polished it up and brought on the funny. I honestly don't know where I'd be without you. Probably living in a studio apartment on the lower east side with five goldfish and a roommate named Blaine. Being with you is WAY better. I couldn't have chosen a better partner in this life.

And finally, to my daughter, Magdalena, who has opened my eyes to the most important things in life. My dear sweet angel, live life fully, with no regret.

Made in the USA
Middletown, DE
21 November 2019